A Fatherless Child

Autobiographical
Perspectives on
African American Men

Tara T. Green

University of Missouri Press   Columbia and London

Copyright © 2009 by
The Curators of the University of Missouri
University of Missouri Press, Columbia, Missouri 65201
Printed and bound in the United States of America
All rights reserved
5 4 3 2 1   13 12 11 10 09

Cataloging-in-Publication information available from the Library of Congress
ISBN 978-0-8262-1821-6

∞ This paper meets the requirements of the
American National Standard for Permanence of Paper
for Printed Library Materials, Z39.48, 1984.

Designer: Jennifer Cropp
Typesetter: BookComp, Inc.
Printer and binder: Thomson-Shore, Inc.
Typefaces: Baskerville and Runic

To the Father and Mother
whom I Honor for loving me

Contents

Acknowledgments

I wish to begin by thanking the student, D. Johnson, who asked the question that inspired this book, and the many students at Southern University in Baton Rouge whom I taught (2000–2003) who continued to inspire me through their devotion to learning and desire to succeed.

As for university support, I want to acknowledge Northern Arizona University for awarding me a President's Diversity and Equity Award Grant (2007) and a Faculty Development Grant (2006) to support my travel to research archives. I also acknowledge the enormous support of my former chair, Allen Woodman, and my friends and colleagues at the university, specifically Deborah Harris (mother to a son), Jennie Durán, Nancy Paxton, and Irene Matthews. I also thank my colleague and friend Eric Otenyo who helped me with my reading of Obama's *Dreams*, my friend Austin Shepard, and one of my former students and a budding scholar, Roland Jackson, who helped me with the research. Lastly, I acknowledge the University of North Carolina, my current academic home, for providing the support needed to complete this project.

Many thanks to the estates of Langston Hughes and Malcolm X for allowing me to quote from their valuable archives. I also want to thank the staff of the University of Missouri Press for all their work.

Thanks to those colleagues and friends who read drafts of the manuscript, specifically Tony Bolden, Dana Williams, Carol E. Henderson, Keith Clark, R. Baxter Miller, and Jerry Ward Jr. And, to black fathers and sons Chester Fontenot Jr. and Jacob U. Gordon, for sharing their perspectives and expertise.

Also, I am grateful to two men of the Flagstaff community, Pastor L. D. Marion and Payton Combs, who talked with me about coming of age in the South, and other members of my Flagstaff family, Minister Arnold and Jeffé Locket, Carrie Combs, Esther Marion, and Gwen Johnson.

I cannot give names, but I acknowledge all of the black men (students, relatives, and friends) who shared their understanding of masculinity with me, particularly as it related to their relationships with their fathers. I shall never forget your honesty, and I honor your trust in me.

Lastly, to my friend Tony Cochran and to my family, thanks for your smiles and support.

A
Fatherless
Child

Introduction

Where Are the Black Fathers?

"I'll never forget the day that my father drove off. I knew I was on my own. I don't want my son to ever have that experience." A black man—an abandoned son and loving father—shares this emotional memory with me twenty-five years after his relationship with his father disintegrated. His eyes reveal a lesson that may be reflected in the autobiographies of black men who have had similar experiences with their fathers: Memories of loss are rarely forgotten. Black men's autobiographies reflect the significance of loss, especially when that loss is the first and most important male role model—the father.

The stories of black men, whether they are relayed in oral or written form, are the inspiration for this work. In particular, my interest is in examining an important issue within black communities that I might have overlooked, had it not been for the voice of one of my former students. While teaching an introduction to African American literature course at Southern University, a historically black university in Louisiana, I was in the process of reviewing background on James Baldwin when a young man asked a question that would haunt me for several years: "Why were so many of these black male writers abandoned by their fathers?" It was a pattern I had not noticed, although I had completed a dissertation on Richard Wright no more than two years before. When I asked him what he thought, he simply shrugged his shoulders and told me it was best for a father to stay in place, even if he didn't want to. This young black man had jolted me out of my oblivion and shown me, in the process, that the question was not merely a literary one, but a social issue that black writers themselves had been trying to answer for decades. My interest in

1

black people, in general, and in black men as my fathers, uncles, cousins, friends, and brothers, in particular, has compelled me to give a voice to what has been a too-often-overlooked subject in literary studies—the impact of absent fathers on their sons. My goal here, then, is to offer an analysis of several "autobiographies" written and published during the twentieth century and ranging from the era of World War II to after the Civil Rights movement (1940–1995). The objective of *A Fatherless Child: Autobiographical Perspectives of African American Men* is to examine the impact of fatherlessness on racial and gender identity formation by looking at black men's autobiographies and other constructions of black fatherhood in fiction by black men. I intend to probe the sons' understanding of their fathers' struggles to define themselves, and, the role of community in forming the sons' quest for self-definition in their fathers' absence. My analysis of the autobiographical works of Langston Hughes, Richard Wright, Malcolm X, and Barack Obama intersects autobiography studies and black masculinity studies, and when appropriate I use cultural studies, psychoanalysis, and sociology.

Autobiographies often illustrate a subject's quest for identity. A book in the genre focuses on a subject that tells about his/her personal experiences expressed though a version of a "self." James Olney argues that an autobiographer, as do people in general, has many selves: "If all selves are unique and, in their uniqueness, only subjectively experienced (i.e. we may experience other selves, but then only as objects, not as proper selves), and [. . .] all selves are constantly evolving, transforming, and becoming different from themselves."[1] Autobiography, then, tracks the transformation of a self as that self constructs a truth that the "self" in relation to the writer desires to reveal to the public.

Of course, truth is a subjective term, which I define as an autobiographer's interpretation of a series of events that is more of a perspective that he or she consciously or subconsciously wants to offer to a reader. Truth is an idea that belongs to both the subjective self who tells the story and the writer who presents the story, and its existence is at the root of tension between the writer and the subject or self. Stephen Butterfield, author of *Black Autobiography in America*, defines the two existences found in autobiography as "a dialectic between what you wish to be-

---

1. James Olney, *Metaphors of Self,* 29.

come and what society has determined you are."[2] Autobiography, then, allows for a re-creation not only of the events that it proposes are factual, but a creation of a subjective "self" known as "I" that knows now what the "I" did not know then. Toni Morrison in her understanding of the differences between autobiography and fiction states, "On the basis of some information and a little bit of guess-work you journey to a site to see what remains were left behind and to reconstruct the world that these remains imply."[3] She suggests that autobiography cannot be an exact truth when memory is involved; it is what is left of the memory, and truth is derived from these remnants. The remnants are then joined together with whatever the writer chooses to provide his contrived subject. As the writer negotiates the contrivance of the self and the truth, the autobiography emerges as a literal manifestation of an accomplishment. Olney also notes, "An autobiography, if one places it in relation to the life from which it comes, is more than history of the past and more than a book currently circulating in the world; it is also, intentionally or not, a monument of the self as it is becoming a metaphor of the self at the summary moment in composition."[4]

In black autobiography, the "metaphor of the self" is rooted in the subjugated self's engagement with racism, as well as in the self's struggle to define himself as a black person in society. Butterfield sees the differences between the self in autobiographies written by white authors and those written by blacks as taking into "account the effect of Western culture on the Afro-American. . . . The self is conceived as a member of the oppressed social group, with ties and responsibilities to the other members. It is a conscious political identity, drawing sustenance from the past experience of the group."[5] Roland Williams Jr. sees the intrusion of racial prejudice as the inspiration for blacks to indulge the narrative form of autobiographies.[6] The black "self" sees himself as part of a group, even when the group may not be present. Kenneth Mostern affirms Butterfield's assertion by observing, "African-American Studies has tended to place autobiography in a relatively stable location in the field:

---

2. Stephen Butterfield, *Black Autobiography in America*, 1.
3. Toni Morrison, "The Site of Memory," 92.
4. Olney, *Metaphors*, 35.
5. Butterfield, *Black Autobiography*, 3.
6. Roland Williams Jr., *African American Autobiography and the Quest for Freedom*, xiii.

where 'I' tends to have a determinate relation to a specifically racial 'we.'"[7] Mostern further argues that the identity of the "self" remains in the "constant and conscious negotiating of the 'I' with a variety of racialized engagements." As I will elaborate, the need to identify with the group is profound, but how the "I" and "we" are defined in relation to each other may change for the black autobiography subject, depending on the author's intent and the era in which he is writing. For the most part, black men's autobiographies show a need to connect with the community, as a racial and cultural group, and their need to do so is greatly illuminated when the fathers are absent. A father's absence makes it necessary for the son to find a place of belonging and to connect with other males in the community who can teach him cultural practices that may be thought of as distinctly black and male. Langston Hughes, Richard Wright, Malcolm X, and Barack Obama prove the need for an engagement within black communities to define themselves as black men, a need made more prominent by the absence of their fathers.

One of the earliest autobiographies written by an African man, *The Interesting Narrative of the Life of Olaudah Equiano, or Gustavas Vassa, the African Written by Himself* (1789), serves as a reminder of the importance of the relationship between father and son as well as the meaning of the loss of that relationship. Equiano describes the familial structure of the Ibo during the transatlantic slave trade. According to Equiano, who is clearly writing to give a human face to the millions of nameless and voiceless Africans who were being routinely kidnapped from West Africa, his father was the head of a family that consisted of at least three wives and several children. Equiano explains that despite the fact that his father held a prestigious position within their community and was the head of a large household, Equiano had a relationship with him that he cherished. It was also his father who gave him a name of special meaning. The family structure may have been different from the European structure, but from the perspective of the African son, the father's presence as the center of the unit was significant and greatly appreciated.[8] This unit is destroyed when the young son is kidnapped, taken from the father

7. Kenneth Mostern, *Autobiography and Black Identity Politics: Racialization in Twentieth-Century America*, 30.

8. Olaudah Equiano, *The Interesting Narrative of the Life of Olaudah Equiano, or Gustavas Vassa*, chap. 1.

whom he admires and loves. African families were separated to satisfy the desires of the slave captors and those invested in the slave trade, and the disregard for African families and their descendants continues well past the Middle Passage into the West Indies and the Americas.

Harriet Jacobs records what had been the state of many black families for decades. To illustrate this point I reference the earliest autobiography published by an African American woman, Jacobs's *Incidents in the Life of a Slave Girl* (1861). Jacobs brings attention to the problem that slave fathers had of balancing governmental authority with natural authority and the results of these fathers' attempts to achieve what was a relationship with their sons that was under constant threat and scrutiny. At a point when her younger brother, William, simultaneously is called by his "mistress" and his father, he chooses to respond to the call of his "mistress," resulting in his father admonishing him. Jacobs recalls, "'You are my child,' replied my father, 'and when I call you, you should come immediately, if you have to pass through fire and water.'"[9] Inherent in Jacobs's father's response is not only his determination to assert parental authority over his son, but also his indignation with the system that makes him less important to his son than a woman who is not his mother but "his owner." Though the son is silently present in this narrative, he, like his father, has surely come to realize that he must learn how to navigate a system that does not recognize slaves as humans and, therefore, intentionally disrupts familial relationships. In short, the father and son are not expected and, in fact, are discouraged from having a meaningful relationship. Their natural bond must be one that they form and maintain as best they can.

At least since the seventeenth century, racist attitudes in society have—with rare exceptions—jeopardized African American fathers' relationships with their children. Scholars vary in their interpretations of the role that slave men were able to achieve as fathers and husbands. It is true that black men were often unable to protect their wives from the sexual advances of white men. According to John Blassingame, there is evidence that many white men realized that liaisons could result in their deaths: "Occasionally slaves killed white men for such acts."[10] An

---

9. Harriet Jacobs, *Incidents in the Life of a Slave Girl*, 210.
10. John Blassingame, *The Slave Community*, 172.

example of resistance is the case of Josiah Henson's father who hit a white man for attempting to rape his wife. Likely as a result of his fear and in an effort to retain his power, the overseer cut off the elder Henson's ear and sold him. Henson's challenge to a white man who threatened his wife provided his impressionable and powerless son with a protest model that Josiah could not have forgotten at the time that he decided to flee slavery. Despite such realities and threats of them, Christopher B. Booker finds, "Black fathers were generally able to maintain their self-respect before their family and community." He notes further, fathers were able to provide their children with extras "by hunting, fishing, and raising gardens."[11] To be sure, at the root of the black son's definition of self is how he perceived his father's definition of him-self as a black man, but the sons can only presume to know what motivates their fathers' behavior. For the father, further revealing himself to the son may mean suffering humiliation, a consequence of American racism. Attaining and maintaining a balance between self-respect and survival was an inevitable and inherent part of parenting for men (and women) of African descent.

As the fathers navigate racism, their children observe (i.e., the narratives of Harriet Jacobs and Josiah Henson), and they come to realize that they, too, are subject to the same rules. How boys interpret their fathers' reactions to racially motivated restrictions on their attempts to enjoy American freedoms results in how they come to define black masculinity. Definitions of black masculinity, as recent scholars have illuminated, are diverse and broad. Keith Clark remarks that "masculinity is based on a socially oriented conception of gender informed by society's obdurate figurations of manhood—ones rooted in strength, power, authority, and heterosexuality."[12] Booker asserts that the most important component of manhood "for African Americans [men] is to earn a decent living."[13] Booker states further, "This is seen as critical to the fulfillment of a man's responsibility to his family and loved ones. As a value its influence impacts other personality characteristics critical to the achievement of man-

11. Christopher B. Booker, *"I Will Wear No Chain!" A Social History of African American Males,* 34.

12. Keith Clark, *Black Manhood in James Baldwin, Ernest J. Gaines, and August Wilson,* 2.

13. Booker, *"I Will Wear,"* x.

hood, such as independence."[14] Much of what these scholars observe is expressed in the autobiographies of black men as they illustrate their struggle to self-define. There is no one true definition of black manhood, but it must be noted that any individual's struggle to define himself should not be stifled, but as any human would want, should be recognized and respected by his environment.

Though there is no "true" definition of black masculinity, some similarities emerge among black men, especially those who matured without fathers. Hughes, Wright, Malcolm X, and Obama express feeling the pressure and responsibility of caring for their mothers, resisting public displays of caring, and stating a desire for needs, especially the need for a loving, noncontentious relationship with their fathers. They indulge the avoidance by finding ways to deal with the pains associated with loss rather than display their feelings by confronting them. Another consequence of fatherlessness leaves them feeling vulnerable to forces they may have identified as detrimental to their status as black men. They ultimately perceive emotional needs as a form of weakness that leaves them further vulnerable. Perhaps in an effort to address these emotions, autobiography becomes a means for the son to confront feelings of vulnerability and to claim a lost power that is associated with the lost father. Not only is the son able to "revisit" the "site" (sometimes mentally and physically) and "reconstruct" the memories of the events described in his autobiography, he is able to have a "conversation" with his father and admonish the elder for deeds that have left the son scarred. As observed by Joseph White and Michael Conner in their reference to Gloria Wade-Gayle's text on testimonies about black fathers and their children, the physical journey parallels the mental as evidenced by "several writers [in Gayles' book] who actively searched for a deeper understanding of their fathers by visiting the communities where their fathers were reared and talked to relatives and friends of their fathers."[15] The reasons for these searches are confirmed by the writing itself, which becomes a tool for healing.

In three of the four autobiographies I discuss—those written by Langston Hughes, Malcolm X, and Barack Obama—the subject searches for a black self in a black community. Clark observes that Richard Wright

14. Ibid., x.
15. Michael E. Connor and Joseph L. White, eds., "Fatherhood in Contemporary Black America," in *Black Fathers: An Invisible Presence in America*, 13.

avoids such a journey. Unlike the other writers, Wright came out of the south and a black community, and as he journeys physically from the south to the north, he does, for he has no choice, reside in black communities from Beale Street in Memphis to Chicago's South Side, but his autobiography, *Black Boy*, seems critical of black communities and their residents. However, his fictional engagements with black communities suggest how greatly he was influenced by them. I agree with Butterfield and Morrison's assertion that black autobiographers see themselves as representing not only a personal experience but that of the race and offer Wright's *Black Boy* as an example of such a dual and personal racialized experience. Inherent in his writing is a communal experience that emphasizes his need to be seen and respected as an individual. I read *Black Boy* as an autobiography that speaks honestly about what it means to be part of a cultural community—as honestly as he speaks about the struggles that black men, like Bigger Thomas, experience in the mid-twentieth-century, post–depression-era America. Notably, nearly sixty years later, Barack Obama will offer an honest depiction of black life in Chicago, taking his cue from his literary father, Wright.

While some recorded their observations of black community living in autobiographies, others did as well through sociological studies. African American sociologist E. Franklin Frazier provides a study of black families in early-twentieth-century rural and urban communities in the North and South. According to Frazier, African American fathers who moved to cities left their families for several reasons, wandering from city to city in search of work or joining the army during World War I. He finds further that families significantly disintegrated under the pressures of city life, when once they were stronger in rural communities.[16] Frazier's findings provide a context for the experiences described in the autobiographies of at least two of the writers, Langston Hughes and Richard Wright, as well as the fictional work of Hughes.

I also see my work in conversation with Keith Clark's recent study of black masculinity, *Black Manhood in James Baldwin, Ernest Gaines, and August Wilson*. While Clark sees community as having a "specifically gendered connotation," with a focus on "black men collectively," I broaden his assertion to refer not only to the men of the community but to the women

16. E. Franklin Frazier, *The Negro Family in the U.S.*, 245.

as well.[17] Community, I believe, for the men who engage it, is a place where cultural practices are present and where there is a sense of belonging for the black man who is in need of understanding himself. In fact, as scholars have argued, the transatlantic slave trade most certainly threatened the viability of black families; however, the African American extended family system remained. Family members and community members, as had occurred in African societies, "took on the responsibility for teaching values that involved collective survival, building harmonious relationships, spirituality, and respect for others."[18] The community's presence is essential to survival and identity formation for the black men I discuss as it provides them with an understanding about blackness and maleness in the absence of the father and despite a mother that is somehow impaired—economically, physically, mentally, and/or racially.

Community is an alternative space that subverts homelessness. Melvin Dixon writes about the meaning of homelessness for African Americans. In his text, *Ride out the Wilderness*, he attempts to "examine the ways in which Afro-American writers, often considered homeless, alienated from mainstream culture and segregated in negative environments, have used language to create alternative landscapes where black culture and identity can flourish apart from marginal, prescribed 'place.'"[19] Black authors—for our purposes, black autobiographers—are engaged in "the search for self and home."[20] Hughes, Malcolm X, and Obama make literal physical moves in search of "homes" where black culture is located. On the other hand, Wright, who was from a black community, has a different relationship with the community, but he continues his search to reconcile his need for self and home. In these communities, the black man is able to develop a definition of black masculinity that is both derived from interactions with the community and imposed on him by the community. While other factors certainly affect his definition of self, the community has a great impact, at least, on how he defines his blackness. Since the father is absent, the community takes his place.

The black men of *Fatherless Child* do not all have the same relationship with their communities. Hughes did not live his childhood in a black

17. Clark, *Black Manhood*, 5.
18. Connor and White, "Fatherhood," 7.
19. Melvin Dixon, *Ride out the Wilderness: Geography and Identity in Afro-American Literature*, 2.
20. Ibid., 3.

community in Kansas, but he later relocated to Harlem to indulge his interest in black folks. Wright, on the other hand, was born in Mississippi and had few options regarding where he would reside; as a result, he spent his childhood and early adult years in black communities. Wright expresses a conflict about his feelings regarding black communities, I argue, because they also harbor what he felt was the tragedy of blackness. His father was unable to rise out of segregated communities, and his mother suffered in one. Though he may see himself as a person who lived beyond the confines of the community, he never truly separated from the community. Malcolm X's relationship to black communities differs from Wright's but is similar to Hughes's. Malcolm X did not live in a black community before his father's death, but he lived in several black communities, including Harlem, from his teen years until his death. Similar to Hughes, Malcolm X sought out black communities where he learned certain cultural practices among black men. Obama was also isolated from black communities during his childhood in Hawaii, and this acute separation seems to have inspired his decision to reside in black communities. He built his relationships with blacks, beginning with a few people he knew, to a group of blacks in college, to a community of blacks in the South Side of Chicago.

Community becomes not only a place where the racialized subject can belong, but it is also a place where the black adult son can begin to heal the pain of having been abandoned by his biological father. By examining the repression of pain in autobiography, I propose that the authors demonstrate the importance of confronting and transforming personal history for the purpose of healing. I observe that healing, in general, is a process where understanding the self as a black person and as a gendered subject occurs. In his father's absence, the black man learns how to navigate in the world partly based on how he perceived his father's success or failure as a black man. Coming to an understanding about the father, in some ways, allows the black man—as we see in the four autobiographies—the ability to embrace his identity. These black men's autobiographies prove that healing is an ongoing process where transformation may occur but is never completed, at least not by the time the autobiographies are published in the men's thirties.

The community, a center for blackness and a location for self-definition, is not always in America. I argue further that these men visit Africa in an effort to further define their blackness. Often, Africa has been referred to as the motherland by African Americans—the place where the race was "birthed." For the black men discussed in *A Fatherless Child,* Africa is the "community" where they can reclaim what they feel was lost to them—an understanding of blackness—when their fathers abandoned them. Their visits allow them an opportunity to determine who they are as black men.

Not unlike the other black men of this study, W. E. B. Du Bois also spoke as an individual for a black communal experience. In doing so, he made the country aware of reactions to racism as a social experience that begins in early childhood. His autobiographical essay "Of Our Spiritual Strivings" is appropriate when considering how, like Du Bois's, later black men's autobiographies describe the writers' reactions, through a critique of their fathers' varying reactions, to treatment as a gendered and racial "other" and how they attempt to overcome this "othering." Hazel Carby has established Du Bois's voice as masculine but not sexist. Carby observes that Du Bois's "I" links him to the black community through the experience of being regarded as a problem.[21] She further observes, "For Du Bois the 'problem' of being black was an issue of both commonality and exceptionalism; it was not just about learning that he was black but also about learning how to *become* a black man."[22]

Significantly, his moment of racial and gender recognition occurs when he is rebuffed by a white female classmate. Carby notes, "This realization disrupts the smooth passage of the formative years of his male adolescence, but the practice of challenging and overcoming such obstacles enables the transition from boy to man."[23] Other black males of the twentieth century would experience the same transition—that is, the struggle of constructing a black male identity when such an identity is seen as a "problem" by dominant society. The four men's autobiographies show the struggle with racial- and gender-identity formation discussed by Du Bois.

Since it is impossible to discuss all of the autobiographies written by black men, I have chosen four that I believe represent well the intersecting experiences of generations (both the fathers' and the sons') of black

21. Hazel Carby, *Race Men,* 30.
22. Ibid., 31.
23. Carby, *Race Men,* 31.

men during the twentieth century, before and after the Civil Rights movement. The Civil Rights movement may also be considered the Black Men's Liberation movement, as black men were called upon to lead the movement and, often, to become its public face. The autobiographies of Langston Hughes, Richard Wright, Malcolm X, and Barack Obama tell not only their own perspectives of certain time periods and various geographical areas during the twentieth century, but also tell of their fathers' lives, as well as they can figure, as black men in America. More specifically, Hughes's *The Big Sea* chronicles his travels to Mexico, West Africa, Europe, the American South, and his placement in Harlem, New York. Born in 1902, Hughes focuses primarily on his coming-of-age during the twenties and in his twenties with some attention given to his childhood. His autobiography was written before the Second World War, and it reflects his concerns with the intersection of race, masculinity, and class, concerns that are directly related to how he perceived his father. Published only five years later, Wright's *Black Boy* differs significantly from Hughes's narrative, offering a critical perspective of America with the subject's travels confined to the United States. Wright's point of view reflects a southern experience tainted by the violent racism he endured in Mississippi and Tennessee. The search for self-definition in a racially hostile society is also a prominent concern expressed by Malcolm X in *The Autobiography of Malcolm X*. Published in 1965, *The Autobiography* reflects the emergence of black men as fearless leaders. Thirty years later, Obama's *Dreams from My Father* answers the call of the Civil Rights movement and Black Power movement by probing the question of what is the role of black men after the movements and in the absence of a national movement focused on black life. Ultimately, their personal narratives overlap as converging voices that speak of the intersections of three generations from the perspective of one voice that is simultaneously personal and public.

The similarities among these four black men of the twentieth century do not end with their race and mode of expression. All of them had troubled relationships with their fathers that I believe they try to understand through the writing, or in Malcolm X's case, the telling, of their personal stories. Their life experiences as expressed in the personal narratives confirm researchers' belief that black males encounter four major challenges "as they move through the life cycle in America: identity, establishing close connections with others, coping with racism, and finding a source of psychological and emotional strength."[24] By the age of five, each man has been abandoned by his father either by flight or by death. Furthermore, the men visit Africa with hope of making a connection there that will lead them to develop their understanding of themselves as "sons" of Africa. Their twentieth-century autobiographies reveal questions that emerged during the slavery era: How does a man define himself as a man in a society that does not see him as human? How can a black father assert parental rights when faced with economic and political challenges?

The following chapters examine the struggles that black men have in constructing and asserting black masculine identities when their fathers are absent. Fathers, through the perspectives of the sons/autobiographical subjects, should be well-respected and highly admired representatives of black men poised to teach their sons moral values, but their absence hinders them from fulfilling their sons' desire in this regard. Most of all, the sons seek to learn how to navigate the world that sees them as a problem because of their gender and race.

In chapter 1, "The Meaning of Langston Hughes's Father-and-Son Relationships," I use Hughes's autobiography, *The Big Sea* (1940) to examine the father/son relationships in his novel, *Not without Laughter,* and his short stories "Father and Son" and "Blessed Assurance." Hughes's fictional sons express a desire for love and acknowledgment from a father who is either emotionally and/or physically distant. In *The Big Sea,* Hughes describes the estranged relationship he had with his father, who lived in Mexico. Hughes's subjective "I" yearns for a racial home where he can reside with and establish a place with the "we" that his father rejects. His search is represented through the "self" who engages the "we" and is motivated by his critique of his father as a lost man whose sense of self Hughes denounces. I argue that Hughes, feeling rejected by his father, seeks within the black community of Harlem a place of belonging or a home where the racialized self can reside.

While Hughes gives more of the sons' perception, Wright focuses more on the fathers'. Chapter 2, "Richard Wright's Fathers and Sons," is an examination of Wright's life as depicted in *Black Boy* (1945) and of

24. Connor and White, *Black Fathers,* 57.

how his perception of his father is revisited in his fiction. In the first chapter of his autobiography, Wright uses the voice of an impressionable "I," named Richard to describe his feelings about his relationship with his father. Wright's attempt to understand his feelings about his father, Nathan Wright, expressed in *Black Boy*, I argue, extends to his construction of his fictional fathers, specifically "Fire and Cloud," *The Outsider*, *The Long Dream*, and the film version of *Native Son*, starring Wright as Bigger Thomas. In showing the complexity of black fatherhood, Wright's fathers strive for independence from social boundaries, and in extreme cases, familial restrictions as well. My analysis, then, includes an examination of how his father influenced Wright's perception of women as seen in his fictional representations of women. Notably, the success of Wright's fathers has much to do with their relationship to the community.

In chapter 3, "Malcolm X's Declaration of Independence from His Fathers," I analyze the perception Malcolm X expresses of his father as an abusive husband, a traveling Baptist minister, and as a Black Nationalist. I rely on what I believe is the authorized biography of Malcolm X, *The Autobiography of Malcolm X* (1965), for it is the closest we will get to a text that tells his perspective about the events that had the greatest impact on his life and, to a lesser degree, his speeches and letters to discuss how Malcolm X came to define black masculinity for a generation of black Americans. His "I" represents the voice of the leader who proposed to speak on behalf of black Americans, particularly black men, of his era. The voice is as intensely personal as it is political. In these personal oral texts, he reveals his perception of his father, who died when he was six years old, and from that story he also reveals how he defined black masculinity through his observations of other black men and especially his surrogate "divine" father, Elijah Muhammad. His relationship with Muhammad marks his shift from the black community as a hustler to a community of black male leaders. What we find is that Malcolm Little/Malcolm X/El-Hajj Malik El-Shabazz, inspired by his father, saw black masculinity as stemming from both spiritual grounding and political ideologies to navigate the social restraints historically imposed upon blacks. The minister was also significantly affected by his father's treatment of his mother, which has a profound impact on him. While Malcolm X's father provided his son with a political framework before his untimely death, his son would also need to advance that thinking by acquiring a spiritual grounding, a way of thinking and being that his father did not possess in the minister's perspective.

In chapter 4, "Barack Obama's Dreams," Senator Barack Obama tells the story of having been raised by his white maternal grandparents; his Kenyan father left him and his mother when Obama was two years old. Obama's autobiography brings readers firmly into a contemporary context of defining blackness in the post–Civil Rights era. He speaks not only from the perspective of a "self" who deliberately seeks an identity as a racialized subject, but also as one who represents the experience of the fatherless "we" in the late twentieth century. Obama raises questions about what it means to be an African American. More specifically, he shows that the Civil Rights movement, where black men came to public prominence as leaders in their communities, and the Black Power movement, where black men came to prominence by striking fear in whites, left young black men wondering: What next? Obama, though a biracial man, consciously seeks a black identity by conversing with blacks and, ultimately, by moving to a black community. Through these engagements, he seeks an understanding of himself as a black man and of race relations in America. *Dreams from My Father* poses a question relevant to black men of his generation: What is my role in post–Civil Rights America?

Chapter 5, "The Sons Return to Africa," is a discussion of why these four men had such a keen interest in Africa that they visited African countries. Their challenges to their black masculine identities in America prompted them to go to Africa in an effort to reclaim a cultural history and identity. Ultimately, these men are trying to reconcile their search for both a home and self. I am interested in their individual interpretations of the African countries and the impact these visits had on them upon their return. Their autobiographies and in Wright's case his travelogue, *Black Power*, which chronicles his travels to the Gold Coast during its transition to Ghana, allowed them to define themselves as men of African descent through an exploration of their relationships with Africa. Based on the political status of the African country each visited, each man had a complex response to Africa that further revealed his double-consciousness. Ultimately, each developed a clearer understanding of himself as an American man of African descent.

I end with conclusions about fathering from a contemporary point of view in "Contemporary African American Fathers and Communities."

Recent debates within the public arena reveal that what was may still be. Clearly, questions emerge and perhaps linger about the state of black men, including their father-and-son relationships. What might we learn from the personal narratives of Langston Hughes, Richard Wright, Malcolm X, and Barack Obama?

Christopher Booker calls for an "identification of persistent barriers to [African American males'] collective development and for shedding light on the process of social change."[25] *A Fatherless Child* seeks to uncover the issues that are barriers to this development but that these authors have, to some degree, identified and overcome. However, they also compel us to consider how much any child can heal from fatherlessness to construct a positive self-image. These four black men are from diverse backgrounds, but their struggles prove to be similar. As long as the barriers exist, questions regarding identity will as well.

25. Booker, *"I Will Wear,"* vii.

Chapter One

The Meaning of Langston Hughes's Father-and-Son Relationships

W. E. B. Du Bois could have been referring to Langston Hughes's *The Big Sea* when he wrote about the "longing to attain self-conscious manhood, to merge his double self into a better and truer self."[1] In *The Big Sea*, the first of his two autobiographies, Hughes reveals the struggle that his father, James, had with "attaining self-conscious manhood"—a status that would have allowed the elder Hughes to live in America as a successful businessman, despite his race. Richard Wright observes, in his review of *The Big Sea*, Hughes's "father, succumbing to that fit of disgust which overtakes so many self-willed Negroes in the face of American restrictions, went off to Mexico to make money and proceeded to treat the Mexicans just as the whites had treated him."[2] James Hughes became an expatriate in Mexico and assumed an identity that established him in a position of power as an American over poor Mexicans. His physical and psychological distance established an irreparable emotional divide between him and his son. Notably, while the father felt it impossible to embrace an identity that would merge the black and American selves in America, Hughes would use literature to affirm a black American identity.

As seen in the construction of the fathers in his fiction and autobiography, when both a father and a son are present, tension between the two emerges which has a major impact on the son's self-definition. Hughes's intimate knowledge of this tension likely motivated him to

1. W. E. B. Du Bois, *The Souls of Black Folk*, 5.
2. Richard Wright, review of *The Big Sea*, 22.

create a definition of a liberated black male self in his fictional construction of his son characters. Hughes poses a recurring question in his literature; it begins in his autobiography and resonates in some of his fiction: What is the impact of a father's absence or presence on his son's quest to attain a "self-conscious manhood?" Hughes's representations of fathers—the power-hungry, the ideal, and the homophobic—illuminate Hughes's concern with the importance of the father-son relationship and its influence on identity construction. In his fiction *Not without Laughter,* "Father and Son," and "Blessed Assurance," Hughes explores the convergence of race, gender, and/or economics and the impact they have on the conceptualization of identity. A theme of his autobiography also emerges in these fictional works: a son's struggle to gain his father's acceptance. In this chapter, I argue that through his occasional fascination with homoeroticism, his indulgence of African American musical forms, and his critique of capitalism, Hughes consistently rejects the definitions of black masculinity imposed by white patriarchy and supported by some black men. In doing so, he advocates a movement toward blackness as derived from his experiences within black communities, a location where acceptance of the black self could be gained and where rejection could be healed.

Hughes's search occurs through the construction of the autobiographical "I" of *The Big Sea,* which is decidedly retrospective and judgmental based on not only the individualized perspective, but one that speaks as a communal voice. To be sure, the community rejects that which rejects it. This voice is identified as Langston. It is Langston who makes the observations and experiences the emotion, but it is Hughes who writes about the experiences and interprets them. Ultimately, while Langston has little control of his environment, Hughes has control of it through his invocation of narrative techniques.

First, in order to understand how Hughes's relationship with his father moved him toward a concern with race, gender, and economics, it is necessary to examine closely the first part of *The Big Sea.* Hughes knew rejection and abandonment fairly early when his father left the country and his mother, Carrie, went in pursuit of an acting career, leaving him in the care of his maternal grandmother. Though his parents made an attempt to reconcile when Hughes was about six years old, the attempt failed when Hughes's mother returned to the United States after an earthquake in Mexico. Hughes was left in the care of his maternal grandmother. Sadly, Hughes did not have a reliable family structure, and he certainly did not have a consistent father figure. After his grandmother died, Hughes lived with his mother, stepfather, and stepbrother off and on through high school. Eventually, his stepfather, like his father, also left the family.

David Dudley asserts that African American men struggle in their autobiographies to establish a hero status that attempts to "persuade [their] readers that [their] own way is the correct path." In Hughes's case, his resistance of an older predecessor "who has pursued that goal by a different means" is prevalent in *The Big Sea*.[3] Hughes is critical of his father, believing he traveled down the "incorrect path" by betraying his racial identity. Although Hughes was not reared by his father, he received a sense of what could be a model of an admirable black man from his maternal grandmother. Mary Sampson Patterson Leary Langston had been married to two courageous men: her first husband was killed in the John Brown insurrection; her second husband was a political and civil rights crusader. Based on their legacies, Hughes's grandmother prompted her grandson to follow in their footsteps. His charge was to uplift the race.[4] Therefore, Hughes learned from a woman and indirectly from other men that a black man did not reject his identity as a black man in America but used his talents and skills to make his place in the country of his birth.

His childhood memories of his father emerge as a blend of his most pleasant memories and his psychic desires. He vaguely recalls his father's "carrying [him] in his arms the night of the big earthquake in Mexico City."[5] His hope for a father who would embrace and accept him clashes with his mother's description of his father as a "devil on wheels. . . . As mean and evil a Negro as ever lived!" (*TBS*, 36). Hughes alternatively had come to envision his father as a "strong, bronze cowboy, in a big Mexican hat, going back and forth from his business in the city to his ranch in the mountains, free—in a land where there were no white folks to draw the color line, and no tenements with rent always due—just mountains and sun and cacti: Mexico!" (*TBS*, 36). Hughes creates a hero

---

3. David L. Dudley, *My Father's Shadow: Intergenerational Conflict in African American Men's Autobiography*, 8.

4. Arnold Rampersad, *The Life of Langston Hughes, Volume 1: 1902–1941*, 5.

5. Langston Hughes, *The Big Sea*, 35, hereinafter cited parenthetically in the text with the abbreviation *TBS*.

image of his estranged father, which includes his hope that the man can give him stability. Yet, James Hughes was angry about his experiences as an American black man, and, as a result, would fall short of his son's expectations (*TBS*, 36).

Hughes's view of his father as a black "cowboy" diminishes almost immediately when the two reunite. Unfortunately, the elder Hughes greets his seventeen-year-old son by asking him why he was not at the train station where he was to meet him, and Langston replies that he did not receive the wire until that morning since they had recently moved. His father's response is insulting: "Just like niggers. . . . Always moving!"(*TBS*, 37). Whether conscious or not, he has in one brief moment called his son a "nigger." And, his tone, as Hughes makes clear, does not leave anything vague by way of interpretation: "he spat" the words out, according to the son (*TBS*, 37). His father deliberately used "niggers" to project a sense of negativity. To his son's dismay, James Hughes has come to define "nigger" as any black person who lives in the United States. James's labeling is the first step in complicating the relationship Hughes seems to want to have with his father as the elder Hughes's attitude clashes with the pride his son's grandmother has instilled in him about the potential of his position as a black man in America.

Langston, likely shocked by these first few moments in their reunion, shows no sympathy for his father in his description. Sociologist Herman Sanders provides insight into the problems of a perception steeped in victimization:

> One's behavior is greatly influenced by one's self-concept. The self-concept is used as a reference point. Self-acceptance or rejection of others are [*sic*] based on one's own concept. Self-acceptance generalizes toward the acceptance of others as a function of degree of self-acceptance, the greater the self-dissatisfaction, the greater generalization.[6]

James Hughes makes a decision to separate himself completely from American blacks and, consequently, he hopes to separate himself from a black American identity. As Langston appears to move closer to un-

---

6. Herman A. Sanders, *Daddy, We Need You Now! A Primer on African-American Male Socialization*, 3.

derstanding his estranged father, he also separates himself from him. As a result, Langston becomes clearer, at least, about the identity he will *not* embrace.

Langston's observation of his father in Mexico allows him to see his father as a man who has successfully assumed an empowered identity that he could not have had in America and to develop a supremacist attitude typical of racists. The attitude emerges through his open contempt for poor Mexicans. Langston recalls that his father called them "ignorant and backward and lazy. He said they were exactly like the Negroes in the United States, perhaps worse" (*TBS,* 40). Hughes writes, "He [James Hughes] thought it was their fault that they were poor"(*TBS,* 41). Hughes describes James Hughes as speaking about the Mexicans like the "other German and English and American businessmen" speak of them (*TBS,* 40). Although James Hughes is among a minority in Mexico, he projects a white patriarchal attitude, as discussed by Christopher Booker. Since the elder Hughes's language is reminiscent of white racists, Langston implies that his father embraces the identity. Langston does not discern any admirable traits in his father. His desire to see his father as a gallant black hero lessens when he learns that his father hates poor people of color, which suggests to Langston that his father hates him.

It is during the first visit that Langston admits that he hates his father, a consequence of constantly being told that he needs to "hurry up!" and finish a task, but he seems to mask a deeper reason for his resentment of his father. Arnold Rampersad observes, "In *The Big Sea,* deeper meaning is deliberately concealed within a seemingly disingenuous, apparently transparent, or even shallow narrative."[7] From Hughes's perspective, not once during his stay did the father seem satisfied with the son's attempts to please him or seem interested in bonding with the son whom he has not seen for over ten years. As a result, except for the time that Langston spent with Maximiliano, "he was depressed and unhappy and board." Eventually, he put a pistol to his head "and held it there, loaded, a long time, and wondered if [he] would be happier if [he] were to pull the trigger" (*TBS,* 47). Langston is beleaguered by what he perceives as his father's primary concern with molding his son into an entrepreneur. Possibly overwhelmed with his father's attempt to spend time with him,

7. Arnold Rampersad, introduction to *The Big Sea,* xvii.

Langston becomes severely ill the morning he is scheduled to travel to Mexico City with his father. He says, "when I thought of my father, I got sicker and sicker. I hated my father" (*TBS*, 49). As a result of his feelings, his stay in the hospital pleases him because he is able to make his father spend money on him, which makes him a priority.

Hughes refuses to characterize this as a moment where the two even come close to having an emotional moment. Instead, James Hughes's concern is significantly ignored by Hughes who vaguely mentions that his father came back from Mexico after four days and that he reserved the more expensive seats on a parlor car to take his son to the hospital. Absent from this are any of the words that must have been exchanged between the two. Hughes deliberately constructs James as a man who is a failure as a father, furthering the reality that they lack the ability to understand each other. Langston thus emerges as a proud hero and his father as a self-loathing villain.

Later, when Langston returns to Mexico for a second visit his father decides that he should go to school to become a mining engineer. The elder Hughes is adamant that his son will not be a poor black American like his mother and other blacks restricted by American racism. When Langston expresses his desire to be a writer, his father reminds him of his race by asking him about black writers who have made money. His desire, he makes clear, is for his son to "learn something you can make a living from anywhere in the world" (*TBS*, 62). James Hughes is not unlike many parents who want to see their children succeed, especially by making a good living. The problem, however, is that he believes that for a black person to achieve economic success he must shun his black identity. More to the point, he appears to equate blackness with oppression: if one is treated like a nigger in America, one is a nigger. Perhaps in rebellion, his son sees beyond oppression. Langston counters his father's ideology: "'But I like Negroes,' I said. 'We have plenty of fun.'" Langston sees himself as belonging to a group and is not discouraged by the political implications and social restrictions placed on the group. His father, on the other hand, does not ignore the deterrents. In this exchange Hughes writes himself into being through the story of Langston's search for a black self and home. James responds, "How can you have fun with the color line staring you in the face?" (*TBS*, 62).

Langston has an appreciation for the color line that his father cannot comprehend. Not only does Langston Hughes's rejection of his father move him closer to embracing black culture and a black identity, but it also encourages him to define his masculinity through a cultural lens that is not corrupted by accepting white patriarchy as the norm. In effect, Hughes's autobiography becomes a tool that seeks to achieve a positive paradigm of black masculinity while rejecting any suggestion that African American men aspire to "a corrosive, severely flawed notion of masculinity that has actually insured their black people's subjugation while failing to confer the desired subjectivity."[8] Simply put, Hughes recognizes his father's identity as a black man as flawed. In his interpretation of James Hughes's offer to support his son if he does not return to the United States, Rampersad notes that he does indeed become a Satan figure—as Langston's mother has described her former husband—who offers his son a European education and access to his wealth if his son will only agree to not live in the United States, where he will be a "nigger," a word that for James is synonymous with black Americans.[9] But, Langston, on the contrary, values African American heritage.

James Hughes exhibits what Sanders calls a "self-rejecting attitude" as a result of his early experiences with American racism. A major problem for him is his inability to reconcile the experiences of his past. While his son was taught that he would become an admirable black man by using other black men, notably his grandfather, as models, it is possible that James Hughes used his grandfathers as models as well. Both men were prominent whites from Kentucky—one a Jewish slave trader and the other a distiller. James Hughes's own father had been born a slave but died an Indiana farmer. His white patriarchs had been successful, and he had hoped to be as successful as they. James was an educated man who had earned two teaching certificates and had passed a civil service exam for the post office. He had also studied law and worked in a law office, but racism prevented him from taking the bar exam. Shortly after marrying Carrie Hughes in 1899, he took a job as a stenographer for a mining company. In pursuit of a lifestyle unencumbered by race, he moved to Cuba. When his venture there died, he moved to Mexico.[10] James

---

8. Stephanie Brown and Keith Clark, "Melodramas of Beset Black Manhood? Meditations on African American Masculinity as Scholarly Topos and Social Menace: An Introduction," 734.

9. Rampersad, introduction to *The Big Sea*, xx.

10. Ibid.; Rampersad, *Life*, 10–11.

Hughes was clearly not only searching for better economic stability, but he was also fleeing the racism of the United States. When he left the United States, he intended to leave behind a country that did not recognize his rights to full citizenship. According to Langston Hughes, James was able to practice law in Mexico, and he became a wealthy businessman. Sanders explains that black men have several reactions to not having access to social equality: laughing it off, playing the clown, resigning, and rebelling.[11] James's reaction, as an expatriate, is to resign.

James Hughes's bitterness about American racism and his inability to define manhood as he wishes within the country of his birth, however, takes a toll on his relationship with his only son. When Langston leaves the United States for Mexico to visit his father for the second time, we can begin to appreciate fully the extent to which he is affected by his relationship with his father. Here the autobiographical self merges with the writer. In a moment of reflection on his father's "dislike of his own people," Hughes writes "The Negro Speaks of Rivers"—a poem that marks the moment when he begins to consciously define his identity, separately from his father's. In this moment—the space between the past and present—he recalls reading that the river he is crossing is where Abraham Lincoln had "made a trip down the Mississippi River on a raft to New Orleans and had seen slavery at its worse" (*TBS,* 54). Then he says he began to think about "other rivers in our past—the Congo, and the Niger and the Nile in Africa" and the words came to him: "I've known rivers" (*TBS,* 55).

Hughes's "I" in this poem connects him to the cultural history that his father rejects. The persona states: "I bathed in the Euphrates . . . . I built my hut near the Congo. . . . I looked upon the Nile. . . . I heard the singing of the Mississippi."[12] He personalizes these experiences, thereby claiming them as his own. The poem also links the "I" to Africa and to the American South. Hughes returns us to Du Bois, the subject of dedication, by displaying double-consciousness. The poem speaks to the endurance of "the black man [who] has seen the rise and fall of civilizations from the earliest times, seen the beauty and death-changes of the world over the thousands of years, and will survive this America" (*TBS,* 55). Ramper-

---

11. Sanders, *Daddy, We Need You,* 4.
12. Langston Hughes, "The Negro Speaks of Rivers," in *The Big Sea,* 54.

sad notes that the poem is "a work that transcends his personal suffering to celebrate the history and beauty of the black race."[13]

"The Negro Speaks of Rivers" marks Langston's conscious choice to embrace what his father denies—an *African* American identity. Langston situates himself as one who is part of a history that is not lost nor is it tragic which is why he "does not understand his father's dislike of his own people" (*TBS*, 54). Further, this poem is a response to his father, a declaration of his racial identity as a "Negro." Rampersad argues that Hughes uses the autobiography to kill his father, "leave him for dead as a mean, selfish, materialistic man."[14] If this is the case, then the process begins with this very first published poem, for it, as Hughes makes clear, is a response to his father's hatred of black people.

After leaving Mexico, Hughes begins developing his black identity by engaging black communities. He admits that his primary reason for wanting to go to New York is to move to Harlem, where he can live among black people. His move there marks another attempt to further his independent identity in defiance of is father. While in Harlem, he is able to not only grow as a writer, but also to establish himself as a black writer among other African American artists of the period. He is also able to attend plays written by black playwrights, visit Harlem jazz clubs, and attend house parties. In sum, he has the kind of fun that he tells his father is celebratory of black life. Of course, Harlem will not be the only black community that he will engage. He will later attend Lincoln University and go on a speaking tour of the black South with Mary McCloud Bethune.

His next step away from his father and toward his own identity occurs when he, after having written to his father that he does not wish to remain at Columbia, journeys to Africa, an act that his father would see as frivolous. For Hughes, his trip to Africa gives him an opportunity to get to the origins of black American identity. At this point in the narrative, approximately five years have passed since Langston admitted that he hated his father and that he had concluded that his father hated himself because he was black. Hughes writes, "I felt that nothing would ever happen to me again that I didn't want to happen. I felt grown, *a man,*

---

13. Rampersad, *Life*, 40.
14. Ibid.; Rampersad, introduction to *The Big Sea*, xix.

inside and out. Twenty-one" (*TBS*, 3, emphasis mine). He expresses pleasure in having found stability not through moneymaking, but by taking charge of decisions that were not influenced by either of his parents, both of whom could have no contact with him while he was at sea. In his article on the autobiography, Brian Loftus observes that Langston's throwing away of the books "figuratively frees him from generic and genealogical constraints as a writer of the text."[15] Hughes is free to construct himself any way he pleases, which may or may not strike a balance between the dialogic truth and the first-person "I." Further, Hughes, through his writing and the adventures of Langston, is free to be black and to expand his own understanding of blackness without having to defend his interests or desires to his father. This may also be the first time that Hughes is part of a group of men who are all of African descent. This group includes his cabinmates Ramon from Puerto Rico and George from Kentucky.

Hughes focuses his literary gaze on George as a hypersexual black male who is hired aboard the ship because the pantry boy had abruptly quit and the steward, seeing George, called, "Hey, colored boy! You, there! You want a job?" (*TBS*, 5). George enters the narrative as a sort of animated, larger-than-life character, rather than a man whom Hughes actually knew. The man from Kentucky shows no knowledge of social boundaries as he lies naked on his bunk, laughing, and threatening his absent landlady with "his appendage" (*TBS*, 5). His is a carefree or, more to the point, careless, attitude about life. George can "tell a thousand tales," "dance a little, shuffle a lot, and [knows] plenty of blues," and perhaps play the guitar (*TBS*, 7). Lotus notes further that George's storytelling represents Hughes's own freedom to "tell a thousand tales."[16] George is poor, southern, and black; as such, he is, for Hughes, an authentic representation of blackness. If Hughes does not invent this man in his autobiography, he certainly reinvents him in his fiction, for example, as Jimboy in *Not without Laughter.*

Hughes writes that Langston and George become good friends, prompting Lindon Barrett to read Hughes's construction of the scenarios of the voyage as homoerotic. Hughes does not describe any sexual

15. Brian Loftus, "In/Verse Autobiography: Sexual (In)Difference and the Textual Backside of Langston Hughes's *The Big Sea*," 144.
16. Ibid.

acts as occurring between men, only between men and women. In these cases, it is through the mentioning of a woman as when George talks about his landlady and as when the African girls are brought aboard that sex with women is associated with violence. According to Langston, in reference to George owing his landlady rent, "he waved one of his appendages around [and said]—she could have what he had in his hand." Lindon Barrett comments that within this space where no women reside, "The discourse of heterosexual braggadocio is invoked in circumstances that unmistakably belie heterosexual possibilities."[17] As fascinated as Langston seems with George's other characteristics listed above, Langston seems even more fascinated by George's comfort with showing himself a man. His nakedness becomes metaphorical, for his threats reveal his need to establish himself as a man—one who possesses power, despite his blighted economic status, which prompted him to accept this job. Further, his threats are toward a woman—his landlady—to whom he is subordinate and whom he is powerless to control, except through a literal insertion of his penis or proverbial assertion of his penis. In *The Big Sea*, there is the lack of attention to the relationships Hughes has with women that he is close to such as Mary and the woman he sleeps with—her apartment which he shares only has one bed—in Paris. Was Hughes gay, bisexual, or asexual? Hughes leaves his autobiographical readers/observers guessing about that just as he does about the identity of Delmar in "Blessed Assurance."

To other men, women are used to affirm masculinity, as Hughes observes. When the ship is docked on the African coast, African girls find their way aboard, and the men indulge themselves, reportedly as a result of having been confined to the ship and not yet given permission to go ashore. The women are there for the men's pleasure, but only if the men pay. Langston observes the men lining up and, in effect, gang-raping the women, as they scream, "Mon-nee, Mon-nee" (*TBS*, 108). Though the plea is ignored, Hughes does not intervene. He says that he goes to sleep. Lotus notes that "Hughes refuses to contemplate the horror and violence of the scene. Instead he subjugates the spectacle to its aural aspect—the young prostitutes' refrain of 'Mon-nee!'—and literally turns his back on

17. Lindon Barrett, "The Gaze of Langston Hughes: Subjectivity, Homoeroticism, and the Feminine in *The Big Sea*," 1.

the rape" (153). It is also possible that Langston feels powerless to stop the crew as they may turn against him.[18] Hughes's persona in this autobiography is consistently that of a quiet observer. He does not overtly address issues that may be disturbing. Instead, he offers descriptions for readers to make their own judgments, no doubt, based on the observations of the autobiographer.

Hughes is able to separate himself from those around him, cast a scrutinizing eye on them, and leave them to the judgment of the readers. In particular, Hughes's descriptions include scrutiny of masculine subjects. Masculinity is defined by the individual, perhaps, but is not free of expectations from the group. George immediately says what he thinks his male cabinmates want to hear about how he will have some power and control over his social status, even while his economic status remains precarious. One man acts toward these African girls, and others follow his lead. But Hughes, the quiet hero, does not act for reasons that he does not make clear. Embedded in his critical observations is that he is among the men, but not of them.

Why Hughes chooses to go to Africa is also not clear, but the choice has many implications. Through his own experiences and observations, Hughes sees traveling as a means by which black men, in particular, can obtain a definition of the racial self. Traveling was an extension of freedom for black men, according to Christopher Booker, who notes that the inability of black men to travel during slavery times was an assault on their masculinity as independent men.[19] Of course, Hughes's father had traveled to define his own masculinity. In a letter to his father, Hughes credits him with inspiring his travels. He tells his father that he did not come to him while he was ill because "I wanted to make my own way in the world—which has proven quite exciting, although I have nothing to show for it except three books and practically know [sic] money. I have travelled [sic] quite a lot, however—as you advised me."[20] He then proceeds to tell him of his trip to Haiti. Innuendos inform the excerpt. First, the son's independence supersedes the management of the father's affairs. Second, he also makes his father aware that money is a distant priority to him. In his two-sentence description of Haiti he

18. I credit R. Baxter Miller for helping me to consider Hughes's dilemma.
19. Booker, "I Will Wear," 23–24.
20. Langston Hughes to James Hughes, letter, June 30, 1931.

speaks briefly of staying in the "shadow" of the "citadel built by the black king Christophe." Hughes illuminates the legacy of the black king as having great import not only to black history, but also to him. Despite being a black man, his father would not appreciate the legacy. Rampersad observes that this trip, in particular his visit to the Citadel, revived Hughes's connection to black culture.[21] Clearly, his trip to Haiti helped him to make his own way. Consequently, he kept a space between him and his father and looked to men of the past to serve as models for the racial identity he had chosen.

Hughes's strained relationship with his father is most certainly revised as it is revisited in his construction of the father-and-son relationship shared by Jimboy and Sandy. Hughes's fiction reflects his attention to black people and their cultural practices. *Not without Laughter* is based on Sandy, a young black boy, and his coming-of-age in Kansas. Sandy is the son of Jimboy, a traveling blues musician, and Anjee, a domestic laborer. Anjee eventually leaves to pursue her husband, and like Hughes when he was a child, Sandy is left in the care of his grandmother, who is the center of stability in his life. The fictional father becomes a flawed but idealistic version of the real one.

Jimboy's most enduring characteristic is that he is a blues musician. As a practitioner of a form of black expression, he is a favorable father in contrast to James Hughes. He brings joy to all but his mother-in-law, and even to her during the brief times he plays religious hymns. The narrator describes his celebration of culture:

> He would amuse himself by teaching [his sister-in-law] old Southern songs, the popular rag-time ditties, and the hundreds of varying verses of the blues that he would pick up in the big dirty cities of the South. . . . He taught her [his sister-in-law] the *parse me la*, too, and a few other movements peculiar to Southern Negro dancing.[22]

For Hughes, Jimboy's celebration of black cultural practices makes him an ideal father. According to Sanders, not only do father-separate children produce idealistic fantasies of their fathers, the usual fantasy

---

21. Rampersad, *Life*, 22.
22. Langston Hughes, *Not without Laughter*, 63, hereinafter cited parenthetically in the text with the abbreviation *NWL*.

includes a father "who has a good time with his family and who is enjoyed by them."[23] Jimboy teaches the blues, an aspect of black culture, to the younger generation. Such instruction will become important at the conclusion of the novel when Harriet (his sister-in-law) will have become a major blues performer and she, in the absence of Jimboy, will be in a position to support her nephew's education. Otherwise, he will have to quit school and get a job to support himself and his mother. Even absent, Jimboy remains culturally connected with his son such that his celebration of culture fulfills his son's desire (though not completely) for a relationship with him and for Sandy to continue his education.

Jimboy's love of travel is critical to his knowledge of black life. He teaches Harriet what he learns from his travels in black communities. Jimboy's ability to engage with this culture draws his son closer to him, as Sandy admires his father's cultural knowledge. Traveling to gain knowledge of cultures, especially those of the African diaspora, was extremely important to Hughes. He traveled to Africa several years before writing *Not without Laughter*, and he later traveled to the South and observed black southern culture.

In fact, the inspiration for Jimboy's "blues education" was Hughes's travels to a southern black community in Louisiana, where he earned a "blues education in New Orleans." The wandering writer took a room on Rampart Street "the leading Negro Street" (*TBS*, 290). On Saturday nights, the second floor of the boardinghouse "was very gay," and there Hughes recalled listening to

> blues records on an old vitrola: Blind Lemon Jefferson, Lonnie Johnson, and Ma Rainey. And sometimes a wild guitar player would come in off the street and pluck a while, providing somebody bought him a drink or two. In Baton Rouge and New Orleans I heard many of the blues verses I used later in my short stories and my novel. (*TBS*, 290)

Hughes's travels not only provided him with the opportunity to engage in black communities, but more important, to see and feel the impact of "a wild guitar player" like Jimboy. These communities made him feel like he was at home—a place where he belonged. Rampersad asserts, as

---

23. Sanders, *Daddy, We Need You*, 10.

a result of Hughes's feeling abandoned by his parents, "He would *need* the race, and would need to appease the race."[24]

Hughes did not have to travel to draw at least one parallel between James Hughes and Jimboy. As noted above, James Hughes was not able to increase his financial status while in the United States, hence he was compelled to become an expatriate in a country where he could do so successfully. Hughes's fantasy father has a similar problem with finding work that does not overburden him. Jimboy is always either physically incapacitated because of the strenuous work, oftentimes the only kind available to black men, or he experiences racial discrimination from his bosses. Sometimes he believes that travel is the only way he can find a suitable job. Jimboy's dilemma returns us to Frazier's findings about black men leaving their families to wonder from city to city in search of work. Hughes uses Jimboy to imply that racism through labor can stultify familial bonds.

In keeping with the fantasy-father paradigm, Hughes constructs a father in Jimboy who is less concerned with money and more concerned with moral standing. When Sandy buys candy with the money that his grandmother gives him to put in the church's Sunday school collection, he lies to his grandmother, telling her that her friend gave him a nickel. But, he tells his father the truth when confronted. The narrator notes, "He couldn't lie to his father, and had he spoken now, the sobs would have come" (*NWL*, 126). Sandy not only respects and admires his father, but the thought of disappointing him makes him feel immediately remorseful. Hughes does not create a perfect father in Jimboy, but he does create a father character who loves his son unquestionably. As a fantasy father, Jimboy "shows very little hostility and does not exert his authority."[25] Consequently, Sandy respects his father, as is shown when Jimboy delicately admonishes his son for theft. The father's words cause his son to want to "escape the slow gaze of Jimboy's eyes, but he couldn't" (*NWL*, 126). Jimboy gives several reasons to his son for acting honorably. First, he addresses his own character strength: "I won't work a lot, but what I do, I do honest" (*NWL*, 127). Second, according to Jimboy, his son's behavior is characteristic of "white folks" who "get rich lyin' and stealin'—and some niggers gets rich that way

24. Rampersad, *Life*, 22.
25. Sanders, *Daddy, We Need You*, 10.

too" (*NWL*, 127). He acknowledges his faults as a man who is frequently unemployed, but he notes that he is an honest man. As one who is more interested in enriching himself culturally than materially, Jimboy stands in stark contrast to James Hughes. Through Jimboy, Hughes implies that one of a father's most admirable traits is his willingness to provide moral instruction with love and tenderness.

Jimboy's departure has a distressing impact on his son, particularly since it puts an abrupt halt to the growth of their relationship. During the summer, when Sandy is happiest, his father teaches him to box and begins teaching him to play the guitar. Elizabeth Schultz observes that the novel is divided by the seasons, and the moods the seasons bring parallel the father-son relationship, including the impact it has on Sandy.[26] Jimboy leaves shortly after school begins, during a critical moment in his son's life. Notably, his departure is on the same day Sandy wants to talk with him about the racial segregation he has experienced, when he and the other black children have been seated at the back of the classroom. With no black man to offer him guidance on how to deal with racism, Sandy is left to navigate on his own. Sandy does not see his father again during the course of the novel.

A new era begins with the school year, marking the profound impact of Jimboy's absence on his son. The chapters "Hard Winter" and "Christmas" highlight the emotional impact of Jimboy's absence. Schultz notes that in these chapters, "In Hughes's complex description of winter, which operates symbolically, psychologically, and unrealistically, it is apparent that nature cannot be neutral in a society permeated by the unnatural circumstances of racism and poverty."[27] Sandy's mother becomes extremely ill and cannot work, which puts the family, who already lives hand-to-mouth, in financial jeopardy. Her sickness seems linked not only with her fatigue and the weather, but also with the absence of her husband, whom she adores. Sandy does not appreciate the absence of his father until he experiences what it is like to desire something that he cannot have and that his father could help to provide. During the cold Kansas winter his greatest material desire is to have a sled. Since his mother is unable to purchase the toy, she asks a family friend

26. Elizabeth Schultz, "Natural and Unnatural Circumstances in Langston Hughes' *Not without Laughter*," 1183.
27. Ibid., 1181.

to build one for him out of some extra boards she finds in the backyard. Sandy rejects the gift that has been made by Mr. Logan, his perceived surrogate father. After he throws a gift from his aunt across the room, his grandmother raps him on the back of the head. Immediately he cries: "Now his pent-up tears flowed without ceasing" (*NWL*, 160). His release allows him the opportunity to lament the loss of his father, whom he desires psychologically, for he recognizes the enormous impact his father's absence has on him and his family.

Jimboy's absence proves that even the fantasy father is far from perfect. Like Hughes's father and stepfather, Jimboy abandons his son and leaves his family to fend for itself. He acts as though commitment to his family is confining. When he is gone, he can party all night without facing familial worry or his mother-in-law's criticism. His need for independence becomes an excuse for his abandonment of them all. Even his act of leaving under the pretense that he is going to join the army makes him a questionable hero.[28] On one hand, he willingly serves his country, thereby embracing an American identity, which Hughes's father felt denied. On the other hand, Jimboy willingly leaves his family, including his young son, behind.

Jimboy's absence also highlights the weaknesses of Anjee, who is characterized as a woman who needs a man; without one—either her husband or her son—she does not do well. She is clearly modeled after Carrie Hughes, who sometimes left Hughes alone to go in pursuit of Hughes's stepfather. From the very beginning of the novel, Anjee's unrequited love for her husband gives her a blues song. She pines over his absences, which include not hearing from him for months at a time. Her emotional dependency on the "rolling stone" husband leaves her son, like Hughes, in the care of her mother. Hughes describes not having a consistent place to live or a family to rely on:

> I had been in the states growing up while my grandmother died and the house went to the mortgage man, my mother traveled about the country looking for my step-father or for a better job, . . . And me growing up with my grandmother, with aunts who were really no relation, or alone trying to get through high school. (*TBS*, 36)

---

28. This scenario, as noted in the introduction of this text, is also cited by Frazier as a reason for homes headed by mothers.

Hughes revises this somewhat. In the novel, Sandy only moves after his grandmother dies; he lives first with his estranged aunt and then with his mother. When he lives with the other two women, loneliness appears as profound in the novel as it does in the autobiography excerpt quoted above. Even before Anjee leaves him in the care of his grandmother to go find Jimboy, his grandmother is his most nurturing parent. In the opening scene of the novel, she protects him from a tornado while his mother is at work. Both his father and, to a lesser degree, his mother contribute to the boy-child's sense of longing.

Not without Laughter represents Hughes's childhood experiences with loneliness and longing. While Jimboy is not a replica of James Hughes, he is certainly inspired by the feelings Langston Hughes had regarding his father's hatred of himself. Through the re-creation of emotions and scenarios, the novel allows Hughes an opportunity to critique his father's self-concept and to further his own immersion in black culture. Notably, the black family is not the primary source for Sandy's well-being. Rather, his sustainability beyond that of his grandmother's love and dedication is derived from black musical forms. It is through black cultural practices such as the blues that Hughes marks as important to the survival of the race.

Four years later, Hughes re-creates the father-son relationship with desire and longing for acceptance at the center. "Father and Son," focuses on a biracial man who is rejected by his white father. Prior to writing this short story, which he would also revise into the play *Mulatto* (1935), Hughes tests the bond of father-and-son relationships in his short poem, "Cross":

My old man's a white old man
And my old mother's black.

. . . .
My old man died in a fine big house.
My ma died in a shack.
I wonder where I'm going to die,
Being neither white nor black?[29]

29. Hughes, "Cross," 58, from *The Collected Poems of Langston Hughes* by Langston Hughes, edited by Arnold Rampersad with David Roessel, © 1994 by Estate of Langston Hughes. Used by permission of Alfred A. Knopf, a division of Random House, Inc.

Hughes's depiction of the "tragic mulatto" as the son of a white father and a black mother, though not an unusual scenario in African American literature, or in American history for that matter, is familiar to Hughes. He reports in *The Big Sea* that his white maternal great-grandfather, Captain Ralph Quarles of Virginia, had several children by his black housekeeper (*TBS*, 12). There were also interracial relationships on the paternal side of his family, and he was often questioned about his racial identity, especially when he went to Africa for the first time and was not accepted by the Africans as black. Issues regarding black identity, Hughes demonstrates, can affect a people for generations. In this case, the sons in the poem, the short story, and the play *Mulatto* struggle to define themselves as both white and black in America.

Before discussing the short story, I would like to discuss the poem, "Cross," wherein the themes of capitalism and identity are intertwined. Hughes's persona begins the poem by showing suspicion toward both his parents, an old white man and an old black woman. In the last line the speaker suggests that race determines identity but that a mixed genealogy poses an identity crisis. His mother is old, black, and poor, and his father is old, white, and rich. As a biracial man, he feels that he has no racial identity. Class differences also surface. Notably, Hughes himself was the child of parents who belonged to two social classes.

In both the poem and the short story, as well as in Hughes's life, father and son are separated by money and power. James Hughes's hold on his son and how he asserted his own manhood were represented by his need to manage every cent of money he made, including what he gave to his son for his educational expenses. In a letter where Hughes responds to his father's request for a record of how he spent money allocated for his educational expenses, Hughes writes, "If you think that [reference to spending money on non-educational expenses], I had rather you give me nothing. Besides, I never like to ask you for funds because I feel that you do not wish, or can not afford, to give them as I know that you care very little about my going to college here and that you are not interested in what I want to study."[30] Hughes appears exasperated in this letter. Although Hughes correlates a personal sickness to paternal hatred in his

30. Langston Hughes to James Hughes, letter, March 2, 1922.

autobiography, he shows in this letter that he continues to desire his father's acceptance of his choices and, ultimately, that he wants his father to show that he "cares." Hughes's longings are projected through his mulatto sons.

The "tragic mulatto" theme represents Hughes's interests in the intersection of racial and gender identity and economic struggles. In his assessment of the poem, James A. Emanuel finds a major theme in "Cross" is the "modern economic discrimination."[31] R. Baxter Miller has noted that the "hidden evil in ["Father and Son"] is capitalistic greed."[32] I advance Miller's reading to include the influences of Hughes's father and son on the construction of Norwood. Hughes's indictment of his father's obsession with accumulating wealth and his belief that his father was corrupted by his obsession with accumulating wealth is manifested in Norwood, the capitalistic, power-driven father in "Father and Son." The short story, set on a plantation owned by Norwood, focuses on the estrangement of a biracial son, Bert, and his white father, Norwood. Bert's mother is a servant to Norwood who has borne him three children, none of whom he claims. James Hughes's conception of himself as a man who is empowered by attaining an upper-class status is challenged by his son in the guise of Bert. While "Father and Son" is certainly an indictment of racism in general and southern lynchings of young black men in particular, Hughes's decision to use the binary connection of father and son illuminates the complexity of black boys advancing into manhood.

Like James Hughes, Norwood relishes his position as a successful businessman and respected member of the community. Consequently, he cannot be a father to the son whom he seems to favor more than the other children. Norwood admits to himself that Bert's "too damn much like me," and in thinking this, he also admits—but only to himself—that the son is his.[33] His curiosity about the boy (whom he had sent off to college) with ways like his causes him to go out to the quarters to have a look at Bert (when the son returns) and to see just how much his son is like him.

31. James A. Emanuel, "The Christ and the Killers," 134.
32. R. Baxter Miller, "The Physics of Change in 'Father and Son," 134. Also see R. Baxter Miller, "A Brief Biography," in *A Historical Guide to Langston Hughes* (New York: Oxford University Press, 2004): 45–49.
33. Langston Hughes, "Father and Son," 210.

Colonel Norwood, conscious of his socioeconomic status and wishing to retain the prestige of his position, responds to any criticism from the men of his circle about how he handles his "niggers" by reestablishing his authority aggressively, and his youngest son poses the greatest challenge. Norwood's ability to wield financial power over the son imbalances the bond. When Bert returns to the plantation an educated young man during summer break, his mother hopes that he can convince Norwood to let him continue his pursuits. But, Bert returns determined that he will not be disrespected by his father. We may recall here that Hughes's fiction emulates his life. Hughes returned to Mexico the second time with the hope that his father would help him to go to college. Although Hughes does not admit to it in his autobiography, he, like Bert, probably returned with hopes that he could heal the strained relationship he had with his father. Bert's reliance on his father causes him to build resentment, which expresses itself first as resistance and, later, as rage.

Bert's struggle to define himself is profound and has much to do with how others define him. Bert learns this as a child. He calls Norwood "Papa" in the presence of other white men, and Norwood knocks him down. Since the father beats him later, the rejection not only has a significant impact on him emotionally, but it also means that he is not allowed to claim the white identity that is a part of his racial makeup. While in Atlanta, Bert enjoys his acceptance into the "colored society." In this venue, he associates with the sons and daughters of Negro doctors and dentists and insurance brokers and professors ("FS," 225). He also dates many black girls of all shades. It is not until he returns to the plantation that he is compelled to resist the stigma associated with being black. He actively and vehemently resists becoming a "white man's nigger," an identity that he sees his brother Sam as having internalized. On the plantation, his father expects him to work in the fields with the other blacks. Bert's rejection of this position probably has less to do with his being treated as a black and more with his rejection of an identity with a lower class of people—those who have to work in fields and make nice with white folks.

Regardless of how Bert feels, southern protocols do not allow violations. He does not acquiesce when the white female postal worker denies his request for fair treatment. Her disagreement with him over how much money he is owed reflects her loyalty to the hierarchy of power: "She looked at Bert—light near white nigger with grey-blue eyes. You gotta be harder on those kind than . . . on the black ones" ("FS," 234). He follows up by wrestling with white men who try to intervene. One of his father's peers verbalizes Bert's dilemma best when informing Norwood that Bert has actually said "he wasn't all nigger no how; said his name was Norwood—not Lewis, like the rest of Cora's family; said your plantation would be his when you passed on— . . . boasting to the niggers listening about you being his father" ("FS," 235). Though he resists them, the white males claim the authority to define him. All of these white men represent a white patriarchal system that is inspired by fear transformed into violence. It is also one that aspires to maintain its status through the accumulation of power, which Bert will never access. In many ways, he tries to emulate these men, but they fear him.

When he returns home and meets the anger of his father, the story can end only one way. It is clear that Norwood will not extend understanding toward his son. In fact Norwood reminds his son of the racial identity and economic status that Bert can never claim. Norwood's position is clear: "To Cora's young ones . . . I gave all the chances any nigger ever had in these parts. Mor'n many a white child's had, too" ("FS," 239). Bert, however, remains adamant about what he has not been given:

"Oh, but I'm not a nigger," Colonel Norwood, Bert said, 'I'm your son."
"The old man frowned at the boy in front of him, "Cora's son," he said.
"Fatherless?" Bert asked.
"Bastard," said the old man. ("FS," 240)

Fearing his son's claim to his power, Norwood pulls a gun but is overpowered by Bert, who strangles him. Rampersad's assertion that Hughes's psychological desire is to kill his own father is demonstrated in this work. The son must kill the father in order to end his own anguish. If one is labeled fatherless, then there's nothing to lose by making it so.

There is no doubt that Colonel Norwood relishes his position as a powerful man, but Bert's greatest flaw is his desire to do the same. Bert fails as a hero because he moves toward trying to attain the identity that would make him rich materially while shunning his own cultural heritage as an African American. His fight with the clerk about the change that he is due and his insistence that he is Norwood's son represent his tragic efforts to navigate a complex identity. While Bert's brother Willie sees himself as a "well-treated" servant on the estate, Bert sees himself—

and is not ashamed to publicize his motives—as the rightful heir of their father's estate and patriarchal identity ("FS," 226). As a result of his misguided needs, the only way Bert can find to empower himself is by defining his own death; he cannot, in other words, define his life.

Dudley's idea that black men's autobiographies speak to an Oedipal desire to replace their fathers is prominent in this short story. Cora occupies herself with a man who depends on her but does not love her. Cora's mother sees the couple's relationship as pleasing since it will bring the children and her daughter a life that is not as harsh as the lives of other blacks on the plantation. But, the problems that come as a result of this union, during the early part of the twentieth century, literally, if not figuratively, as in the slavery era, seem to exist over the heads of Cora and her mother. First, Cora does not raise her own children since she lives in the Big House with Norwood. Consequently, Bert learns in the fictive world, as do Frederick Douglass and Booker T. Washington and so many others in actual history, that his father is the plantation owner not from the father himself or from his mother but from someone else on the plantation. In this case, Bert learns from his grandmother. Second, though Norwood allows "Cora's niggers" to attend school, he does not allow them to enter the front door of the house or step foot on the porch; he treats them as he treats the other blacks on the plantation. Bert sees both his parents, knows who they are, but does not enjoy a familial relationship with them and, in fact, is kept from them both, especially his mother, who seems to put her relationship with Norwood before that with her children. Hence, the son's bitterness toward both expressed in "Cross."

Not until the end of the short story does Cora acknowledge that her role as Norwood's mistress is less important than being her son's mother. After she realizes that Bert has killed Norwood, she goes to her room and makes a place for her son to sleep under her bed, thereby offering him protection. She also goes so far as to proclaim that Norwood was not welcomed into her room, but of course, these actions are too little, too late. Now that the son has displaced the father, he has his mother's undivided attention. She also regrets having earlier followed Norwood's command to bring Bert to the house, knowing that the two were at odds. Cora is sadly weak. At no point do we see her acting before Norwood's murder to protect her children from his wrath. Rather, her sudden breakdown in the wake of her lover's death and her son's pending lynching shows her privileging patriarchal power over maternal love. Hughes's construction becomes an indictment of the father and the lifestyle he represents, as well as of the mother and her indulgence of the lifestyle.

"Father and Son" features a corrupt cast of characters. At the core is the man, Norwood, who has defined his identity in a society that regards a man as one who can govern the actions of those who are deemed his subordinates on the basis of their social, political, and economic status. Anyone who enters into this space has no choice but to follow the historical script. Bert's racial makeup is his cross. Away from the plantation he enjoys a life as a black man among blacks, but his return to the plantation reminds him of his white father's rejection. Cora's decision to become part of the system as a willing lover of Norwood allows for the creation of further corruption. While she may have been sexually exploited, and Bert may be mistreated, all are culpable. Hughes makes clear that a move toward a white patriarchal identity produces a failed African American identity.

Unlike in the other two stories, where both the father and son are featured prominently, Hughes makes prominent the father's perspective in "Blessed Assurance." In this 1963 short story, Hughes focuses on a father's fears that his son is a "queer." The story is told from the viewpoint of John, the father of Delmar, a choirboy of about seventeen. This time the narrative strategy leaves the child's consciousness unnarrated.

John's suspicions about his son are based solely on his definition of masculinity. The father believes that because his son does his "chores without complaint," plays with dolls, does not play sports, and holds his cigarette between his thumb and finger—"like a woman"—that surely he must be homosexual.[34] John has established a clear definition of how boys and men should act. He looks to his son to rebel and not do his chores. He does not want his son to do anything that his daughter does, such as play with dolls. Ultimately, he also wants his son to show masculine roughness by playing sports. In short, a man should hate all things defined by other men as feminine.

John's observations lead him to narrow conclusions, allowing him to overlook an important fact: Delmar is a rebel. When Delmar sings at

34. Langston Hughes, "Blessed Assurance," 374, hereinafter cited parenthetically in the text with the abbreviation "BA."

church, he takes the lead normally sung by a woman "without respect for gender" ("BA," 375). His father, overwhelmed by the possibility that his son is a homosexual, does not consider the fact that his son sings the part only because he has the vocal ability to sing in the prescribed key. In fact, Delmar brings to the community of black churchgoers a cultural experience that they otherwise would not have since the church is northern and bland. Anne Borden asserts, "The ironic twist of Delly's academic and personal success suggests that in breaking from traditional styles of masculinity—sexually and socially—Delly avoids certain traps which defer dreams for young boys trying to fit into 'proper' gender roles."[35] His ability to do this allows him the ease he needs to define himself as a young black man irrespective of how his father would prefer that he define himself. If he is gay, it does not matter, demonstrates Hughes.

John reasons that he fears that homosexuality is an additional barrier for his black son. To be young, gay, and black spells certain destruction in American society. Hughes writes, "Since colored parents always liked to put their best foot forward, John was more disturbed about his son's transition than if they had been white. Negroes have enough crosses to bear" ("BA," 374). That he has excelled in his school, is looked upon by the black community as wholly acceptable because of his talents, and is looking to study outside the United States at a prestigious university means that his race does not completely confine him. But a primary personal obstacle is that he does not have the full acceptance of his father.

From the time he reconnected with his father until James Hughes's death, Hughes remains conflicted about their relationship. However, Hughes stayed in touch with his father after James Hughes became extremely ill and after Hughes became a well-known writer. In a letter to his son dated January 13, 1931, the elder Hughes expresses confusion about *Not without Laughter.* He inquires about Sandy and Jimboy: "It is very amusing; it breaks off without telling what was made of Sandy or what finally became of Jimboy." He proceeds by advising his son about his artistic style, his finances, and women. The elder Hughes tells him to dispense with "Negro dialect" and to "try to use good English so that people can see that you are capable of doing it." Twice he tells his son

35. Anne Borden, "Heroic 'Hussies' and 'Brilliant Queers': Genderracial Resistance in the Works of Langston Hughes," 333–46.

that he hopes that he is saving his money. Finally he tells him to protect it from "some nigger wench." Further, "if you ever get married get a woman that has been brought up in the washtub, and knows, at least, how to wash and iron your and her own clothes."[36] Hughes responds, "If I make a lot of money from my next book I will come down and see you. . . . Thanks for all the good advice. I'm sure you're right."[37] At this time, Hughes was no longer dependent on his father. Earlier letters were dialogues about money that Hughes might have owed to his father who was in better health. But by this time James Hughes was dependent on his son for companionship and for a connection to the United States. And he certainly did attempt to connect with his son by reading his work and offering commentary on the work. Judging from the son's sedate reaction, Hughes appears much calmer and accepting of the familial distance. Ironically, the distance that remains between Sandy and Jimboy at the end of the novel, which James Hughes questions, is visible in the men's relationship as well. Did James Hughes know this when he asked his son about the ending?

Hughes's literature proves the importance of loving black father-and-son relationships. Langston Hughes's desire for his father to love himself as a black man and to accept his son as a black American man emerges as a prominent concern in his autobiography and extends to his fictional as well. His literature reveals his love of blackness that perhaps is largely owed to his father's need to critique Hughes's racial pride while simultaneously defining himself as an empowered African American man beyond the confines of American racism. While they could not agree on what it meant to be a black man, both rejected the imposition of limits and restrictions based on their race.

36. James Hughes to Langston Hughes, letter, January 13, 1931.
37. Langston Hughes to James Hughes, letter, June 30, 1931; excerpts from letters reprinted courtesy Harold Ober Associates.

Chapter Two

Richard Wright's Fathers and Sons

Richard Wright's autobiography, *Black Boy,* tells of a son's inheriting responsibility for his family when the father abandons it. Influenced by the author's experiences, Wright's literary sons struggle emotionally to survive economic burdens and social barriers. While Wright certainly endured the long-term effects of paternal abandonment, *Black Boy* also reveals his observations of other men who might have been father figures but were not: his Uncle Silas Hoskins, whose courageous defiance of the rules regarding economic prosperity for blacks so frightened the white men that they killed him; his grandfather, a Civil War veteran who is too old to be much of a threat to his precarious grandson; and his mother's brothers with whom young Richard remains constantly at odds. Silas also appears to have been the model for the Silas character in Wright's "Long Black Song."

Despite the presence of the other men in Wright's childhood, Wright consistently uses his estranged father as inspiration for his father characters, even when they appear more respectable than the man he describes in *Black Boy.* Regardless of their reliability, all his father characters have one experience in common: Their experiences illuminate mid-twentieth-century black men's struggles for recognition as humans with full citizenship rights. Haki Madhubuti writes about the challenges black men endure when defining their position in America. He states:

Most often we have had to navigate life through the worldview, ideas, culture, systems and prejudices of others that has forced many of us into mediocrity, a blinding hopelessness and destroyed a good percentage of us. Being born Black, male and developing into Black manhood is often, in America, a dangerously paralyzing journey.[1]

What is absent from Wright's *Black Boy* is a father who assumes the role of "guide" on the journey Madhubuti describes. Through the experiences of young Richard, Wright shows the importance of fathers finding a balance between their struggle with racial oppression and their responsibility to their families.

Most attention to the fathers in Wright's work has been on *The Long Dream.*[2] However, one of the most intriguing father-and-son relationships is described in the first chapter of *Black Boy.* In that chapter, we learn of the repercussions of the troubled relationship between young Richard and his father. In fact, in earlier drafts of *Black Boy,* Wright wrote in more detail about the troubled relationship he had with his father. As shown in *Black Boy, The Outsider, The Long Dream,* and "Fire and Cloud," the son's relationship with his father affects his ideas of manhood, especially how he perceives women.

Black Boy stands as Wright's attempt to understand his feelings about his father, which emerge in his construction of his fictional fathers in "Fire and Cloud," *The Outsider, The Long Dream,* and *Native Son,* the movie.[3] *Black Boy* is an example of a black male self's voice that speaks for and about the racial community. Wright associated his father with the limits of black communities that were largely formed by segregation. Abdul R. JanMohamed observes that "the inability or unwillingness of the father to protect him from racial assault leads to an adamant negative association between the father and black culture in general" (144). Wright desired to see himself as one who could move beyond social limits, but his literature shows that he is never fully separated either from the community or from his father. Further, Wright does not hold the community accountable for his father's failure, and his fictional fathers show the pos-

1. Haki R. Madhubuti, *Tough Notes: A Healing Call for Creating Exceptional Black Men,* 16.

2. Some of these scholars include Katherine Fishburn, *Richard Wright's Hero: The Faces of a Rebel-Victim* (Metuchen, NJ: Scarecrow, 1977) and Elizabeth Yukins, "The Business of Patriarchy: Black Paternity and Illegitimate Economies in Richard Wright's *The Long Dream," Modern Fiction Studies* 49 (2003): 746–79.

3. Hereinafter citations will appear parenthetically in the text with the following abbreviations: "Fire and Cloud," "FC"; *The Outsider, TO;* and *Black Boy, BB.*

sibilities of engagement with the community. Ultimately, Wright's socially powerless fictional father figures challenge any notion that economic and social barriers inevitably lead to black men's inability to be responsible fathers. In showing the complexity of black fatherhood, Wright's fathers strive for independence from social boundaries and, in extreme cases, familial restrictions as well. By examining the repression of pain in his autobiography, *Black Boy*, and in his fictional fathers, I propose that Wright's fiction demonstrates the importance of confronting and transforming personal history for the purpose of healing.

Since *Black Boy*'s publication in 1945, debates have raged about its status as an autobiography. The truthfulness of several scenes have been questioned by his biographers. One such scene is "Uncle Hoskins and the Mississippi River," where Uncle Hoskins scares young Richard when he drives their coach into the riverbank. According to biographer Constance Webb, this happened not to Wright but to Ralph Ellison, who told the story to Wright.[4] However, more recently, Hazel Rowley finds the incident to have likely occurred as relayed by Hoskins's son, Fred, who recalls his father driving him into the middle of a pond in Mississippi, having the effect of scaring him as well.[5] Fred Hoskins's voice as a black man serves to vindicate Wright and to authenticate Wright's autobiographical voice and, by extension, his assessment of his environment as he observed and critiqued it. According to Wright, *Black Boy* is not simply a true story about his life: "An autobiography is the story of one's life, but if one wants to, one can make it more than that and I definitely had that in mind when I wrote the book." Wright does not deny that *Black Boy* is an autobiography (and more), as he goes on to state, "I wrote to tell a series of incidents strung through my childhood, but the main desire was to render a judgment on my environment."[6] This environment is the South, where "[under]nourished Negro human beings" live.[7] James Olney argues that "the bios of *Black Boy* is Richard Wright's past life, his past experience, his existence as 'Richard' or as 'black boy.'"[8]

4. Constance Webb, *Richard Wright: A Biography*, 305–6.
5. Hazel Rowley, *Richard Wright: The Life and Times*, 13.
6. Keneth Kinnamon and Michel Fabre, eds., *Conversations with Richard Wright*, 64.
7. Ibid., 65.
8. James Olney, "Some Versions of Memory/Some Versions of Bios: The Ontology of Autobiography," 247.

Olney captures what Wright intended by layering a story that casts him as the subject of an experience in a given historical moment and space—the Jim Crow South—but autobiography allows for the past to be assessed in the present by a man removed from that space who can interpret those events as he chooses. For him, autobiographical writing allows him to access and assess the impact of the events on him, his parents, and others—black and white—whom he encounters. Autobiography also allows Wright to attain and assert power that his child's voice did not have but desired.

My concern is not with the accuracy of either the dialogue or of the nuances of what he claimed to have seen, but rather with *Wright's perceptions* of what he says occurred and why he gives life to these perceptions. It is clear that Wright found writing necessary to the very act of living. Through writing he was able to negotiate his status in an environment that he perceived as antagonistic, including the racism of the South, the estrangement of his father, the dependence of his sick mother, the religion of his grandmother, and, over it all, the specter of poverty that dominated his childhood. The black boy remained in constant need.

Through young Richard, Wright's retrospective biographical persona, Wright conveys his interpretation of his father and, by extension, reveals his emotions as related to his father. He begins his introduction of his father by describing him as a man with a "huge body which slumped at the table" the result of eating "long and heavily" (*BB*, 11). Then, according to young Richard's observations, he would sigh, belch, close his eyes, and let his head "nod on a stuffed belly" (*BB*, 11). Immediately, food represents what is lacking between father and son. Robert Felgar observes that a "dominant theme in *Black Boy* is hunger—hunger for food, life, love, knowledge, opportunity."[9] But Wright reveals that hunger goes beyond even these desires: "As the days slid past the image of my father became associated with my pangs of hunger, and whenever I felt hunger I thought of him with a deep biological bitterness" (*BB*, 18). Wright's association of hunger with his father's absence illuminates how he uses writing to attempt to understand and alleviate his "father hunger"—a

---

9. Robert Felgar, *Understanding Richard Wright's "Black Boy": A Student Casebook to Issues, Sources, and Historical Documents*, 2.

term that Evelyn Bassoff describes as a son's "deep craving for physical and emotional interaction with his father . . . and the loss and emptiness felt as a result of being deprived of such interaction."[10] The father is cast as a man who sits alone and hoards sustenance while his son looks on; between the two there is no bond that flourishes through communication, only two beings that exist alone. He concludes that he "was the lawgiver in our family and I never laughed in his presence." The child sums up his feelings about his father in one sentence: "He was always a stranger to me, always somehow alien and remote" (*BB*, 11). Young Richard's feeling of emotional rejection from his father is likely the beginning of the "I" that always seems alone and at odds with his family.[11]

Young Richard tries to fill the void of the relationship he has with his father by provoking his father's anger. When Nathan Wright shouts at his son to kill the stray cat that he and his brother had brought into the house, Richard finds a perfect opportunity to challenge the lawgiver, the man who seems to take up too much space in the family's home. As a result, he follows his father's instructions and kills the cat. Young Richard admits that he kills it to make "his father believe that he had taken his words literally" (*BB*, 13). He regards his act of defiance as a triumph (*BB*, 13). There are two probable reasons for young Richard's defiance: he has a strong need to get his father's attention (but he does not get it, for it is his mother who makes him take responsibility for his actions); he has decided that he does not like his father. Young Richard's need to use words to show the elder Wright his hatred is indicative of Wright's writing of *Black Boy*. The work itself seems largely an attempt to address his feelings about his father as the foundation for the feelings that emerge in his life after his father leaves. The son seeks the one way available to empower himself by attempting to force his father to have an emotional response toward him. In other words, he kills the cat to make his father feel his pain. It is clear that while he fears his father, he has a strong desire for paternal acknowledgment and love.

Undoubtedly, then, the event that had the greatest impact on Wright was his father's decision to abandon the family. Though young Richard

10. Evelyn Bassoff, *Between Mothers and Sons: The Making of Vital and Loving Men*, 95.

11. I am referring here to the fight he has with his aunt, the tension between him and his Uncle Tom, and the relative absence of his younger brother in the narrative.

presents himself as a boy who closely observes his father's eating habits, he says he does not notice his father's absence until, significantly, he realizes he is hungry. When he tells his mother, she says, "You'll have to wait. . . . For God to send some food." To make her point clear she asks her son, "Where's your father?" (*BB*, 17). Their exchange forces young Richard to confront a situation that he has chosen to ignore, and even at his young age he realizes that his father's absence marks the end of their relationship and the beginning of physical hunger and psychological hunger for his father's presence. When Nathan Wright leaves he threatens his son's opportunity to eat as well as any hope his son has of having a relationship with him.

As a direct result of his father's absence, young Richard, who is about five years old and the older of the two sons, must take on greater responsibility for his family. It may be at this time that "he learned that men could not be trusted."[12] He describes two scenes in which he is thrust toward manhood. First, young Richard's mother finds a job as a cook and must leave her two sons alone while she is at work. She tells them that they must learn how to take care of themselves for they have no father and their lives will be "different" from those of other children. Thus, he says, "they felt a vague dread" (*BB*, 18). Soon he is responsible for doing the family's grocery shopping. On the first afternoon when he undertakes this task, he is beaten by a gang of boys and robbed. His mother, reminding him of his new responsibility, sends him back with the warning that if he returns without the groceries, she will whip him. The child completes the task by blindly swinging a stick at the boys and running wildly at them. Young Richard is thrust into a community that meets him with hostility, and his father is not present to guide or protect him. His only choice is to lash out against the community. If he does not, the family cannot eat. His responsibility to feed his family is a reminder that his father is gone and that he must fill the void of his father's absence. Despite his reluctance, young Richard is taking his first step toward manhood, and his father's absence causes the event.

Through young Richard, Wright furthers his assertion that his father's desertion (in)directly contributed to all the tragic events of his miserable childhood. Young Richard recognizes yet another effect his father's ab-

12. Rowley, *Life and Times*, 7.

sence has on his mother, and subsequently, on him: "After my father's desertion, my mother's ardently religious disposition dominated the household" (*BB*, 30). She is seeking another father/provider/protector for herself and her two sons through the presence of God who is represented by the preacher his mother invites to Sunday dinner. Young Richard observes the man eating too fast and too much, and he declares: "That preacher's going to eat *all* the chicken!" (*BB*, 31). The preacher's act of eating the food young Richard perceives as his and which he has not seen much of since his father's desertion, is metaphorical as well as physiological. The preacher is a threat to him for two reasons. Young Richard likely associates the preacher with his father who also wanted to become a preacher. And, like his father, the black man eats without restraint. As a result, Richard perceives them as two Bible-reading black men who fill their bellies at *his* kitchen table. Young Richard feels that his family is threatened by the man who could become his father's replacement, erecting a barrier between mother and son. More important, at this time in young Richard's life, food is scarce, and the preacher, like young Richard's father, completely disregards the child's physical hunger and other needs to satisfy his own desires. Ultimately, young Richard battles against loss.

It is his loss or, more precisely, his abandonment—the fear of and the reality of it—which remains consistent in this book, growing even more prominent when Ella Wright becomes ill and leaves her sons at an orphanage. However, her guilt and the boys' constant complaints, along with young Richard's attempt to run away, prompt her, eventually, to remove them from the home. Wright describes the "boy's" feelings: "During the first days my mother came each night to visit me and my brother, then her visits stopped. I began to wonder if she, too, like my father, had disappeared into the unknown" (*BB*, 34–35).

Black Boy is an emotional narrative, a story about a young boy's perception of and relationship with his parents. Young Richard knows that his mother is doing all she can to provide for him and his brother: "My mother hated to be separated from us but she had no choice" (*BB*, 35); however, judging from Wright's description, he did not get over what he felt to be his abandonment in the orphanage. Young Richard's separation from his mother is more complex because it is forced upon both mother and son by circumstances beyond their control. Evelyn Bassoff notes further,

Less fortunate little boys, [those who do not have fathers to turn to when they choose to separate from their mothers] however, grow up feeling that they can turn to no one; having relinquished the comfort-giving mother [in Wright's case, forcibly relinquished] and finding no comfort from father, they may go through life believing that they must bear all their hardships alone.[13]

Finding himself without a home and a father at the age of seven, young Richard experiences feelings of vulnerability and powerlessness.

Unfortunately, even when given the chance, his father does not attempt to alleviate his son's suffering. According to Wright, his father remains consistent in denying his son. At one point, Ella Wright takes her estranged husband to court in order to extract family support. Upon hearing from Nathan Wright that he has no money, who claimed, "I'm doing all I can" the judge does not order him to support his family (*BB*, 32). Wright remarks, "It had been painful to sit and watch my mother crying and father laughing" (*BB*, 32). His father, by not accepting his responsibility as a father, is not a man but a grinning "black boy." The Mississippi judge allows him to assume this identity—one that the judge likely preferred. He states further that he did not hate his father but "simply did not want to think of him" (*BB*, 32). Through his description of the incident, Wright critiques the court system that does not support the family, especially the welfare of growing young black boys. He further notes how his father indulges the system that on one hand abuses him (e.g., institutionalization of Jim Crow laws), and, on the other hand, allows him to be derelict in his responsibility. Claudia Tate states that unconscious desire "can produce textual meaning, which in turn complicates the explicit social message of the text."[14] Wright's decision to "render a judgment on his environment" is not exclusive of American racism but is inclusive of all those who participate in the oppression of black children.

A second step toward manhood occurs when his mother asks him to speak on the family's behalf for financial support. Wright describes an emotionally charged scene where a son faces his father. Both young Richard and his mother stand in front of his father and a "strange

13. Bassoff, *Between Mothers and Sons,* 56.
14. Claudia Tate, *Psychoanalysis and Black Novels: Desire and the Protocol of the Race,* 9.

woman" who laughs at him. Further denying any responsibility for his family, the father says that he has no money. Young Richard witnesses the exchange as he feels the heat from a fire burning in the fireplace. As is Wright's style, he paints a remarkably colorful picture overflowing with raw emotion. The "strange woman" tells his father to give him a nickel because he is cute. The child rejects the nickel and, subsequently, his father. He extends his rejection of his father even further when he threatens to kill the elder Wright with a fire poker—a proverbial staff of judgment. The setting for this scene—a room where the temperature is hot, resulting from a blazing fire—is appropriate. It is for the son a hell and his father whom his mother condemns: "If there's a god, he'll pay you back" is nothing short of Satan incarnate (*BB*, 39).

This scene has implications beyond young Richard's rejection of his father. Scholars have concluded that his depictions of women have been mostly influenced by the women who dominated his childhood, his mother and grandmother.[15] While I agree with their arguments, we must also consider the impact of his father's behavior on Wright's perception of women. The women of his early childhood are his mother, an abandoned woman who is too sick to care for her sons independently, and his father's mistress, who aids his father in the degradation of the family structure. These depictions of black women in particular beg important questions that Wright implies in his autobiography and fiction: Who is to blame for the father's decision to leave his son? Is it his mother and/or his wife? There is a tension between men and women, husbands and wives, mothers and sons which is prevalent in his work. As they mature, boys receive their instructions about women from men, whether it be their fathers, father figures, or the men on the corner. In Wright's case, he receives instruction from his absent father, the one who left his family financially destitute and went away with another woman. It is no surprise then that Wright is drawn to "strange women," or promiscuous ones, such as Bess with whom he has sex in Memphis and the young, illiterate woman with whom he has a sexual affair when selling insurance.[16] Ironically, though he is complicit in their immoral behavior, he is

15. See Claudia Tate, *Psychoanalysis;* Tara T. Green, "The Virgin Mary, Eve, and Mary Magdalene in Richard Wright's Novels," *CLA Journal* (December 2002): 168–93.

16. Rowley finds that Wright had a sexual affair with "Bess" (*Life and Times*).

repelled by the weakness in their moral character. Wright has several affairs even after he becomes a father and a husband.[17]

Yet, he seeks to not become the man he perceives as his father. In a rare instance in the autobiography, Wright interrupts the past by removing the child's mask and allowing his voice as the writer and adult son to emerge. The author fast-forwards twenty-five years to visiting his father, who was by then a sharecropper. Wright observes, "I could see a shadow of my face in his face, though there was an echo of my voice in his voice, we were strangers, speaking a different language, living on vastly distant planes of reality" (*BB*, 40). Wright recognizes his father as having struggled against a society that impeded his humanity by not giving him a "chance to learn the meaning of loyalty, of sentiment, of tradition" (*BB*, 41). His is, as Wright earlier stated, an alien existence devoid of emotion and ability to form meaningful connections and communications. At this point, Wright appears to make an effort to understand the man who abandoned him by crediting his father's failures to a racist society, represented by the fact that his father remains "chained" and "fastened" to the plantation that he attempted to leave by going to Memphis, but instead he remained confined by social restraints (*BB*, 41). With these sentiments he states further, "I forgave him and pitied him" (*BB*, 41). And though he may be telling the truth, pity does not allow him to overlook the "scalding experiences" that marked his childhood (*BB*, 41). David Dudley's assertion that African American men in their autobiographies struggle to establish a hero status in resistance against an older predecessor is demonstrated.[18] To be sure, Wright constructs himself as a hero who can critique his father. Wright describes his father as a "toothless" old "black peasant" one who lacks "understanding" and has "failed" as a father and a husband. He relishes the fact that in stark contrast to his father, he has moved far beyond the plantation. In an effort to prove and define his manhood, Wright resists his father's model, and his literature is a manifestation of his resistance.

Notably, in order for him to reach these conclusions he had to return to Mississippi. Wright, through the guise of Bigger, revisits his communal location in the movie version of *Native Son*, cowritten with Pierre

17. See Rowley, *Life and Times.*
18. David L. Dudley, *My Father's Shadow: Intergenerational Conflict in African American Men's Autobiography,* 8.

Chenal. Before telling Max why and when he killed Bessie, Bigger describes a dream that includes Bessie. As Bigger, played by Wright, attempts to bury evidence linking him to Mary's death in an area outside a cotton field, Bessie appears and tells him that he cannot bury it there and should bury it "out yonder" in the cotton field. As Bigger follows her directions, he sees his father standing in the middle of the field, wearing overalls.[19] The man extends his hands to Bigger, and Bigger tells Max that his father's presence made him feel as though nothing would happen to him. However, his father abruptly transforms into Mr. Briton. Feeling betrayed by Bessie, Bigger kills her, only to learn from Max that she did not betray him. Bigger's anger at his father is manifested through his murder of Bessie who is available in proximity when his father is not. He projects, then, what JanMohamed terms as a "social-death" that emerges as a "figurative and rhetorical death" common among Wright's fathers.[20]

Bigger's feelings of betrayal by a woman whom his mother condemns as not good enough for him, even though Bessie has a job and is seeking elevation in society by engaging in a singing career, returns us to the misogynistic themes of Wright's body of work and his portrayal of women. It is not at all clear why Bigger's mother finds Bessie disagreeable, but the answer surely lies in Wright's consciousness, as is suggested by Bigger's dream. Undoubtedly, Bessie is a manifestation of the strange woman who Wright does not name in *Black Boy* but who was a coconspirator of sorts in betraying his mother and family. She is an enemy set out to destroy the family, which Bigger himself is supposed to protect. Hannah Thomas, Bigger's mother, tells her son that he must be a role model for Buddy because he has no father. Therefore, the mother makes clear that the eldest son must assume the role of the father/protector.

It is surely notable, however, that once Bigger learns that she was not the one who reported his whereabouts to the police, he apologizes for killing Bessie. This is a significant moment, one that serves as a moment of redemption for both Bigger and Wright in his revision of the novel

19. The image of the man is reminiscent of a picture of Wright with his father taken to record the meeting described above. See Fabre's pictures of Wright in his biography.

20. Abdul R. JanMohamed, *The Death-Bound-Subject: Richard Wright's Archeology of Death*, 145.

that made him a nationally known writer. If Bessie's murder in the novel only sealed Bigger's (mis)identity as a sociopathic serial killer, the murder of Bessie in the film gives him a humanistic quality. Through this act of killing a black woman, and not through the act of killing Mary Dalton, he sees himself through a different lens and is therefore elevated to a state of mental freedom.

Previous to this moment, Bigger remains in need of the protection and love of the father who was killed in the South. On at least two occasions it is mentioned that the father was killed by whites. Killing here is symbolic not only of a kind of literal death with which Wright's work remained concerned in regards to the treatment of black men in America but also recalls Wright's need to protect himself by emotionally separating from his father, whom Wright perceives as having physically and perhaps emotionally separated himself from Wright. Given these tragic realities, it is no wonder that he retains a need to feel protected by his father, to feel his loving touch. Consciously he realizes that this will never be an act of fact. Further, his feelings of paternal abandonment and betrayal by his father, even if as he believes his father's actions are somehow motivated by racism and economic barriers.

The barriers, however, cannot hinder the son's development. Both revisits in the autobiography and the film to the most southern of black communities—a cotton field—are moments akin to healing marked by retrospection and forgiveness. Tate observes, "Wright realized rather early in his career that writing was therapeutic" (109). She goes on to note his interest in psychoanalysis as "an intellectual pursuit or as methods of creation and characterization" (110). Accordingly, before 1944 and the publication of *Black Boy* in 1945, he became a participant in a psychoanalysis exercise when he and analyst "Frederic Wertherman conducted 'an experiment in the free association of ideas in the relationship between writing and psychoanalysis'" (110). These exercises in understanding the subconscious through writing are also attempts to heal or to alleviate the emotional burdens that have developed as a result of the events that lie in the memories that Wright sought to explicate. *Black Boy* is a tool for exorcising the demons that Wright harbored regarding his father. Wright's expanded memory of his father when Wright is an adult and an accomplished writer is his attempt to understand the circumstances that would compel his father to abandon him. Further, whatever he understands about his father clearly becomes the motivation for not abandoning his own children. His attempt to redefine fatherhood through the reconstruction of admirable black fathers continues in his fiction through his construction of black fathers.

One such father is Rev. Dan Taylor of Wright's first collection of published fiction, *Uncle Tom's Children*. "Fire and Cloud" focuses on the struggle of a father whose dignity is linked to his need to achieve independence from social forces, which he has allowed to define his masculine identity. The story is set during the depression. Taylor is the pastor of a church in a southern town of about twenty-five thousand people, and as he tries to determine how he will appease the mayor, be a leader in his community, and maintain the respect of his son, he is approached by two Communists who want him to endorse publicly a march for hunger relief. Like Wright's own father, this father is affiliated with religion; however, Taylor's call not only to the ministry but to action does not go unfulfilled. Taylor will teach his son that he can define his manhood despite racism, and the community is the location where he is able to uplift himself and be a model to his son.

Reverend Taylor is a male leader who is seeking to define his position even as others try to define it for him. The members of Taylor's church beg him to help them feed their crying babies since their requests have been met with threats of imprisonment by the local government. For the most part, the community looks to Reverend Taylor to act as their provider of both spiritual and physical instructions. The women look to him as a "father" for their children, a man they expect to ensure that their children will eat. They desire that he serve as a "Direction giver," a characteristic Madhubuti sees as part of manhood, but Taylor's claim to power is challenged by his internal insecurities and external expectations.[21] The black community meets with him in the basement while the Communists and the mayor wait for him upstairs. Reverend Taylor's mental state is manifested in his literal movement from one level of the house to the other. The location of each of the players in this drama of poverty and oppression shows the position of these people in society. The community is at the bottom, and those who have claimed power and are asserting it are above them.

Taylor's decisions are under close scrutiny by the mayor, the Communists, and by his son, Jimmy. Wright does not make clear how old

21. Madhubuti, *Black Men*, 6.

Jimmy is, but he is old enough to want to organize a group of his friends, encourage them to arm themselves, and to show the "white folks" that they are men. His father is the one who gives him the lessons that he needs to not only survive in their society, but to make decisions that will be the most effective in his and the community's fight for survival. Therefore, he discourages his son's move toward violence: "Yuh fixin t git us all inter trouble now! . . . Yuh gotta be careful!" ("FC," 163). Reverend Taylor impresses upon his son the importance of taking responsibility for others and not indulging his own innate desires.

While Taylor contemplates his dilemma, he also remains hopeful that his relationship with his heavenly father will bring him the independence from the mayor that he wants. He recalls that God had called him to save his people like he had called Moses. In the face of adversity, he is confused and scared. He also feels that God has left him. Notably, the reason Taylor feels abandoned is because his vision is distorted by a hegemonic gaze: "now the whole thing was giving way . . . right before his eyes. And every time he tried to think of some way out, . . . he saw wide grey eyes behind icily white spectacles" ("FC," 160). Not only has Taylor allowed himself to become the mayor's agent, he has also lost his sense of himself as God's servant. Wright suggests that servitude of any kind stunts the profile and progress of black men. Reverend Taylor must define himself independently of what others expect of him and in terms of what he expects of himself.

Self-definition, then, will come only when he can answer an important question: Who is he? Taylor sees himself as a man who rose from the fields to attain prominence as a leader of his people. He also hopes that he has the respect of the mayor and other town officials. In order to maintain this particular illusion, he seeks a way to appease everyone, to avoid trouble, and to be everyone's favorite man at the end of the day. He does not want to be identified by the white folks "as a bad nigger stirring up trouble" ("FC," 160). JanMohamed describes Taylor as "overwhelmed by his habitual acquiescence to white domination, which induces the belief that blacks cannot successfully assert themselves."[22] His preoccupation with what white men will think of him gives them the power to define him. But on the day the action of the short story takes

22. JanMohamed, *Death-Bound,* 64.

place, he learns that it is impossible to please everyone. He must then decide whether he will continue to appease the mayor by remaining his faithful "nigger."

Reverend Taylor's struggle is rooted in the fact that he has allowed himself to become the mayor's Uncle Tom. Wright begins *Uncle Tom's Children* with his description of an Uncle Tom—a label that "denoted reluctant toleration for the cringing type who knew his place before the white folk" (*UTC*, preface). Following his observation is a collection of short stories, which redefine the post–Civil War definition of "Uncle Tom." Harriet Beecher Stowe's novel, *Uncle Tom's Cabin*, made popular the figure Uncle Tom. He was a loyal, Christian slave, dedicated to serving the Christian needs of his master. Wright's collection is a response to Stowe's novel, through revising the identity of this early black man, who was constructed by a white woman. Dan McCall notes, "In calling his book *Uncle Tom's Children*, Wright refers us to this mystic father [Uncle Tom], makes his characters the progeny of a stereotype and brings his book into the family of protest literature. These children are different. They refuse to be like a father, an object of pity."[23] McCall's statement brings to surface a prominent theme of Wright's autobiography: a son's refusal to emulate his father. Through Reverend Taylor, Wright will have him assert a masculine identity, including taking care of his responsibilities and maintaining his dignity.

Only when Taylor is confronted violently by white men is he able to assert a black masculine identity. He transforms from a black man who perceives himself as powerless to one who will embrace power through action. During the whipping, "He turned over; it came to his back again, *whick!* He stopped struggling and hung limply, his weight suspended on arms he could not feel. Then fire flamed over all his body; he stiffened, glaring upward, wild-eyed" ("FC," 200). In response to their whipping him, he declares, "We'll get you." This proclamation begins his transformation. He no longer thinks in terms of what is best for him, but he now thinks in terms of a communal and powerful "we." As they continue, "he dropped his head and could not feel anymore" ("FC," 201). He has reached a breaking point. When Taylor awakes, he soon finds that he is not the same man who was taken into the woods. The pain

23. Dan McCall, *The Example of Richard Wright*, 24.

that he suffers is not simply physical; it is humiliating. According to Jan-Mohamed, he undergoes a "social death," which he follows with a re-birth experience that is "politically more efficacious."[24] As a result of this near-fatal confrontation in which Reverend Taylor is forced to realize that his humbleness does not garner respect, a new identity emerges. The father is transformed into a man of confidence at the point when he makes a decision that is solely his own. Most important, it is not the de-cision to protest the treatment of the poor people in his community that empowers him, but the fact that he made a decision that has redeemed his manhood.

Taylor proceeds by imparting wisdom to Jimmy, whose own under-standing of his position as a black man is shaped by his interpretation of his father's actions and reactions. Therefore, his task here is to teach his son how to be a black man in a society when being one can result in that man suffering from brutal violence and perhaps death. As a result, the conversation Reverend Taylor has with Jimmy after the beating allows his son to learn how to be a man and how *not* to be a man. Taylor must first move past the humiliation of having been beaten by other men, a humiliation he feels during his attempt to explain his decisions to his son: "Fire seethed not only on his back, but all over, inside and out. It was the fire of shame. The questions that fell from Jimmy's lips burned as much as the whip had" ("FC," 206). Speaking becomes a necessary part of his transformation. He confesses that his way of life was not productive: "Ah done lived all mah life on mah knees, a-beggin n a-pleadin wid the white folks. N all they gimme wuz crumbs!" ("FC," 209). Taylor finally admits that he has been oppressed and has allowed oppression to occur. His next step is to confess to his son that he was beaten by other men.

From his father's honesty, Jimmy will learn that men are fallible. Hav-ing learned from his own mistakes, Reverend Taylor explains to his son the importance of working with the community to achieve a goal and that there is more than one way to claim power. He does not abandon God but believes that belief in God alone is useless: "Gawds wid the peo-ple! . . . All the will, all the strength, all the power, all the numbahs is in the people!" ("FC," 210). He shows his son the possibility of community action by assembling his congregation and by marching despite more

24. JanMohamed, *Death-Bound,* 64.

threats of violence. When the mayor summons Reverend Taylor to him, Taylor's act of rejecting the mayor's request shows that he now fully sees himself as a man and not as a "nigger." It also shows his willingness to assert his manhood without fear. The result is success. From his father, Jimmy learns how to be a dignified black man, independent of the definitions imposed by others.

There are some similarities between this short story and the other works in which a son, a father, and a mother are present. Taylor's wife, May, is a whiny black woman. When she learns that the Communists have come to visit her husband at the same time the mayor is waiting for him and he asks for her help, she begins to cry. Then she exclaims: "Don do nothing wrong, Rev. Taylor, please! Don fergit Jimmy!" ("FC," 171). A logical response may have been to ask her husband what was going on and to offer her support. Instead, she worries her husband to the point that her anxiety becomes yet another burden that he must shoulder.

Further, the father sees the woman as one who needs their son to look after her and not the other way around. On one occasion he tells his son to "go see bout yo ma" because she is upset about the demonstration. Wright clearly sees one aspect of manhood, even if imposed on him by the women in his family, as taking care of women; in particular, the son in the father's absence must be able to lend his strength to his mother in her moments of weakness. In these instances, fathers and sons always appear as heroes in striking contrast to the mother. While the depiction of the father-and-son relationship is admirable, the depiction of the mother, especially in contrast to those of her son and her husband, is troubling.

"Fire and Cloud" features a man who meets his son's needs, allowing the son to see a model of a black man who finds the courage to successfully navigate social and economical barriers. More important, his acquisition of power through the emergence of a self-identity does not compel him to abandon his son but rather to embrace him. On the other hand, Cross Damon of *The Outsider* shows what can occur when a boy develops into manhood without a loving father. *The Outsider* is about Cross Damon, a twenty-six-year-old black father and husband, who seizes an opportunity to begin a new life under an assumed name when he finds out that the authorities have named him among the people who died in a train accident. Cross's unresolved father issues are manifested in his relationships with women and in his inability to form an emotional bond with his own sons.

The influences of Wright's responsibility as provider for his family (mother, brother, grandmother, and, later, his wife and daughters) are prevalent in *The Outsider*.[25] In this novel, Wright depicts the anxiety that fatherlessness has on a man who is the only son and child of a woman embittered by her failed marriage with his father. Like Wright at Cross's age, Cross feels the burden of being his mother's son. Further, he feels repressed by the presence of God, his mother's perceived spousal replacement, as we see in *Black Boy* when the child protests the preacher's presence. The narrator says that as a response to having an absent husband, Mrs. Damon "took her sorrow and infant son to God" (*TO*, 28). From that point on, she apparently let God be the ruling force in both their lives. Her religion has such a prominent presence in her life that she names her son Cross "after the cross of Jesus" (*TO*, 29). However, his last name, Damon, meaning demonic, describes his repressed identity and his innate ability to deceive by assuming any identity.

Cross has many identities. As a son, he endures a troubled relationship with his mother whom he perceives as having an obsessive relationship with God. Consequently, he rejects God as a manifestation of his father, the man who abandoned him first as an empty presence and later through death. Further, the narrator finds that

> [Cross's] first coherent memories had condensed themselves into an image of a young woman whose hysterically loving presence had made his imagination conscious of an invisible God—Whose secret grace granted him life—hovering oppressively in space above him. His adolescent fantasies had symbolically telescoped this God into an awful face shaped in the form of a huge and crushing NO, a terrifying face which had, for a reason he could never learn, created him, had given him a part of Himself. (*TO*, 22)

Cross sees his mother and God similarly. Each is one entity, a force that is both loving and oppressive but at the same time is responsible for having granted him life. Yet, the entity is not female, but male ("had given him a part of *Himself*"). Significantly, the identity of the woman is superseded by that of the male as creator. Without consciously recogniz-

---

25. For more information about Wright's family life before and during the writing of *The Outsider* see Rowley, *Life and Times*.

ing it, he sees God as a father figure and a presence that cannot be ignored. Thus, this father figure, or God, remains prominent in Cross's interactions with his mother and with others, especially women. His mother speaks not simply as a woman but as one who is deeply entrenched in the emotional trauma resulting from her relationship with a man, Cross's father. As a result, Cross's relationships with women are always judged by the impact of the emotionally tragic events of his mother's past, a legacy that is exclusively his.

His mother projects upon him the harsh feelings she has about men in general—feelings she has harbored since her marriage to Cross's father. Even after her husband's death, she remains unhealed of the pain she endured as a result of his extramarital affairs. Cross has come to see himself as a stand-in for his father and further believes that his mother imposes her emotions for her husband on him: "She was blaming him somehow for [her marriage] having gone wrong, confusedly seeking his masculine sympathy for her sexually blighted life" (*TO*, 21). The repercussions of "his mother's incestuously tinged longings" had the impact of "linger[ing] with him for days" (*TO*, 21). Mrs. Damon is unable to allow her son to emotionally separate from her, and he feels overwhelmed by her "incestuous" connection to him. Her son feels as though she places upon him the emotional weight of her failed marriage. Bassoff comments on the harmful affects of such experiences: "It is usually women who have been treated abominably by significant men in their lives who vent pent-up feelings of rage, fear, or contempt against their innocent male offspring."[26] *The Outsider* mirrors *Black Boy*, the emotional narrative of Wright's life. In both, we find the adult son of a religious mother who feels overwhelmed, indeed overburdened, by his mother's emotional dependence, which is caused by the father's absence.

Although women are present in the novel, *The Outsider* is intensely male-centered and black community–based. In the opening paragraph, Wright states, "On a Southside Side street four masculine figures moved slowly forward shoulder to shoulder" (*TO*, 1). During the dialogue that follows, we learn that the "masculine figures" are black male postal workers who are longtime friends. Cross is part of this masculine community but feels a longing to move beyond it. Significantly, the men have accepted him as

26. Bassoff, *Between Mothers and Sons*, 75.

one of them, but he has not accepted them. In fact, Cross clearly is in a situation that he desperately wants to escape. Cross has fallen into "traps" because of his longing to fill an unidentifiable void. We can infer from the conversation he has with his friends that he has read numerous books because he "was looking for something." But he confesses that he does not know what that "something" is (*TO*, 8). Cross rejects the community of black men, tolerates them at best, and does not feel as though the community that has accepted him is fulfilling his needs. If this void is ever filled, it is filled when he assumes the identity of another man in an effort to escape his life, including his responsibilities as a father, son, and husband. In order to escape his life, of course, he also has to separate himself from his community.

In addition to his troubles with his mother and his estrangement from his friends, he cannot maintain a favorable relationship with women. More than in his other works, in *The Outsider*, Wright draws a parallel between the impact of paternal abandonment and the son's relationships with women. As a result of Cross's emotionally challenging relationship with his mother and the model of his adulterous, drunken, absent father, Cross is unable to commit to any black woman he engages. For Cross, women are the enemy. Since he feels he was manipulated into marrying Gladys, Cross has several affairs during the course of their marriage, including one the night their first son is born. After they separate, Gladys rightly insists that Cross provide for her and their sons. Since Cross has felt trapped from the onset by this marriage and his family, it is no surprise that he moves to sever the ties. Cross assumes an alternative identity—a masked transformation—to end his relationship with Gladys. He probes his consciousness to devise a plan that will force her to evict him from their house, for his other plans to provoke her anger have failed. He thinks that he needs a plan that is not a criminal act but a psychological one (*TO*, 72). By wearing the mask of a cold, insane man, Cross "unknowingly" and abruptly slaps Gladys twice on two separate occasions, causing her to draw a gun and demand that he leave. Cross has decided that as long as he financially supports his family he is fulfilling his obligation as father and husband. Therefore, his actions are justified. He further shows his inability to expand his idea of manhood beyond financial support by placing the "decision" to end the marriage on his wife. It was her fault that he was a husband and a father, and it will be her fault that he has to leave his post. Cross's relationship with his wife reflects that of his parents. Like theirs, his is marred by emotional turmoil and the husband's desire to leave. Extramarital affairs and alcohol become means of escape from the life these husbands and fathers do not want.

As Gladys probes her own memory of Cross slapping her, we see a side of Cross that we will not see again: his role as a father. His son enters the room and tells Cross that he is hungry. The narrator says, "Cross swept the boy up in his arms and fondled him. . . . Cross burrowed his head playfully into Junior's stomach and the boy giggled" (*TO,* 80). The attention that Wright gives to the son's request for food and to Cross's playing with his stomach returns us to the theme of hunger or a need for a paternal relationship prevalent within Wright's father-and-son relationships. Christopher B. Booker's assertion that the most important component of manhood "for African Americans [men] is to earn a decent living" and is linked to a "fulfillment of a man's responsibly to his family and loved ones," aptly describes Cross's understanding of fatherhood.[27] Wright demonstrates that financial provisions cannot take the place of active engagement. Significantly, although Junior tells his father that he is hungry, it is his mother who goes to make his breakfast. When Cross abandons them, Junior will indeed know hunger for he will experience father hunger. Cross later says that his sons will not miss him because they are not close anyway (*TO,* 196). This scene contradicts his thinking, which is clearly an attempt to convince himself that fulfilling his desire to leave his life is more important than his obligation to remain.

Not only is he separated from his wife and his sons, he is also trying to sever the ties between himself and his young mistress, Dot. Though he clearly made a decision to be with Dot and even pursued her, he blames her for their relationship and the negative feelings he has developed in response to the relationship. The narrator identifies Cross's feelings about women and their "hold" on him,

> All his life he had been plagued by being caught in relations where others had tried to take advantage of him because they had thought him supine and gullible; and when he had finally confronted them with the fact he knew that they were playing him, they had hated him with a redoubled fury for his having deceived them! And he dreaded that happening with Dot. (*TO,* 37)

27. Booker, *"I Will Wear,"* x.

Women only become his enemies after he uses them as distractions. Cross's mistress is a black teenager who is neither intellectually nor emotionally compatible with her adult lover. During their first meeting in the liquor section of a department store, Cross fondles her left breast with his elbow. She does not protest and later engages in a sexual relationship with him, all the while leading him to believe that she is seventeen.

The narrator describes Dot as "a passionate child achingly hungry for emotional experience. . . . He would try to talk to her and as he talked he could tell that she was not listening; she was pulling off her dress" (*TO*, 41). Dot perfectly fits the description of the illiterate girl an older Richard sleeps with while he is an insurance agent: "I could not talk to her. . . . Sex relations were the only relations she had ever had; no others were possible with her, so limited was her intelligence" (*BB*, 341). Sherley Anne Williams notes, "Though she is a passionate child, Dot has little of that 'terrible simplicity' that characterized Bess Moss and the nameless illiterate of Wright's early days in Chicago."[28] Like Richard with the nameless illiterate, Cross is able to talk to (not with) Dot. Eventually, Cross's relationship with Dot leads to a pregnancy for which he is unwilling to accept responsibility. Dot threatens suicide to get him to remain in a relationship with her but to no avail. Dorothy "Dot" Powers uses her sexual prowess against Cross. She obtains legal counsel and tells Cross's estranged wife and his elderly mother about her pregnancy. As a final tactic, she threatens to use the fact that she is only fifteen to get charges of statutory rape filed against him.

Dealing with a series of dilemmas, all of which are associated with women, causes Cross to want to be the man he could have been and the man he wishes that he were. He blames his wife for interrupting his pursuit of a philosophy degree at the University of Chicago. In his view, his plan to become a teacher was disrupted by meeting Gladys, her pregnancy, and his need to care for his family, which resulted in his taking a job as a postal worker. Since he has a responsibility he does not want, his job at the postal service is a metaphor for that burden. He tries to relieve the pressure by drinking heavily, which at times makes him sick enough that he can avoid work by calling in sick. Cross's present life is not his life, at least it is not the life he would like to acknowledge as his. In a sense he

---

28. Sherley Anne Williams, "Papa Dick and Sister-Woman: Reflections of Women in the Fiction of Richard Wright," 411.

is an alter ego of his self—an alternative identity that has been imposed upon him by the circumstances of his life and the expectations of others.

These circumstances lead to his longing for death, but it becomes obvious during the subway accident that he really wants to live. Death for him means that he does not want to continue to live the life that he has been living. When he finds that he is pinned down in the subway train he goes through great lengths to free himself and to leave the scene of the accident, including hacking at the head of a dead woman that is hindering him from freeing his legs and stepping on the face of another dead person to lift himself out of the train. Further, after he leaves the train station and has a drink, he does something he has not done for the two-day duration of the novel. He goes to eat. Almost immediately, before he makes the decision to allow his family and friends to think that he is dead, he admits that he wants to live. However, his act of not eating the breakfast shows that he is not yet ready to make the step into living. What he hungers for cannot be satisfied until he fully engages the process of identifying what he desires the most. Cross later realizes that his "wish is a hunger for power, to be in command of oneself" (*TO*, 196).

Freedom is the path to the power he longs to possess. As he contemplates the possibility of remaining dead, he thinks, "All of his life he had been hankering after his personal freedom, and now freedom was knocking at his door, begging him to come out" (*TO*, 107). Freedom means that he must also convince himself that he has no role of real significance to his family other than to care for them, and the insurance money will fulfill that need. His great desire for independence returns us to Booker's assertion that another personality characteristic critical to the achievement of manhood is independence, but independence from his family does not make Cross a man, Wright will show. Cross has a distorted view of manhood. By seeking the freedom from his mother's, wife's and mistress's needs, he can totally extricate himself from any psychological hold the women have over him and any emotional feelings he has for his sons. He also walks away from the community of black men and will later secure his decision to separate himself from them by killing Joe. Movement toward a new identity and a new life will take form as a matter of process. First he witnesses his burial; then he moves to another city; and finally, he will assume the name of another black man.

Regardless of what he names himself, Wright makes clear that Cross is still a father and thus condemns the behavior of a man who abandons his responsibilities to his children. After living as Lionel Lane, Cross Damon is confronted with his past identity when district attorney Ely Houston tries to force him to admit that he is, or at least was, Cross Damon. To achieve his goal, Houston summons Damon's wife and three sons to identify Lionel Lane as husband and father. The idea of summoning family to identify a man who does not, for all intents and purposes, want to be identified compels readers to consider the motives of this scene. On the surface, we see Damon, a man who remains determined to not be outwitted by his admirer, nemesis, and fellow outsider, Ely Houston. But on the other hand, the black man who sits in the custody of Houston is also struggling not to be overpowered by a system that attempts to define his identity. However, Houston succeeds in doing just that through this confrontation. Cross can either claim the family that he has and offer an explanation, or he can act as though he does not know them. He chooses the latter, for his desire to be an independent man who is not subject to emotion is of the utmost importance to him. Like Nathan Wright in the Mississippi family court, Cross Damon rejects his responsibility as a father in the presence of his sons.

Ultimately Houston is the character who can offer explanations for the protagonist, since only Houston—himself an intellectual and physical "outsider"—has intimate knowledge of Cross's motives. He does this when he assesses Cross's final act of abandoning his family:

> "Are you going to let them remember you all of their lives like this? Boys love to think of their fathers as strong, wise men. To many a son the image of his father is what lifts him up in life. A father can make a boy feel that he has a sure foundation under him, can give him confidence" (*TO*, 521).

Cross was not given this by his own father, nor was Richard Wright. As Houston suggests, the cycle will continue with Cross's three sons, who witness not only their father's rejection of them, but also the pain this rejection causes their mother. Wright successfully suggests in this novel that parents' actions have a direct impact on their children, as conveyed through the circular motion of *The Outsider.* The son (Cross) is unable to have a healthy relationship with his mother. Their relationship is haunted by a drunken, adulterous, absent father who is the perceived source of his mother's emotional reliance on her son. As a result, he is attracted to women whom he perceives as needy and naïve, and when he feels overwhelmed by their dependence on him, he flees. The cycle continues as the son is unable to have committed emotional relationships with his wife and children. This pattern will likely continue with the sons whose father is now absent—first through an emotional detachment which allows him to abandon them and finally at his death.

If Wright does what David Marriot suggests, kills his own father through emotional separatism in his autobiography *Black Boy*, then he certainly does the same to the father who abandons his sons in *The Outsider*.[29] Cross's ability to turn his back on the most important responsibility he has—to be a father to his sons—makes him a failure. His desire for independence comes at too high a price when the result is to inflict emotional damage on his sons. Not only has Cross abandoned his family, but he has also separated himself from his black community of family and friends in Chicago. The result is that his racial and masculine identities have been compromised. He does not seek a life beyond what will satisfy his own selfish desires. Cross's physical death, then, represents his failure as a father and ultimately as a black man.

While Cross Damon willingly leaves his black community, including his sons who will have to learn to live with the scars of paternal abandonment, in Wright's novel *The Long Dream*, a father relishes his position as a guide to his son and as a powerful though corrupt figure in the black community. After noting that Wright has been criticized for his "inability to present a living, functioning black community," Paul Gilroy goes on to note: "However, *The Long Black Dream* presented a total, dynamic black community."[30] The novel centers on the relationship between Fish and his father, Tyree, a corrupt mortician who also owns a brothel and a club. In her article on the novel, Elizabeth Yukins argues, "Tyree Tucker plays a formative role in developing Fishbelly's consciousness and in shaping the central themes of the novel: embattled masculinity, the economics of racialized patriarchy, and the sexual psychology of racism."[31] Though Tyree is married to Emma, a Christian woman, he has affairs with other women, including the prostitutes in the house he owns, and he has a

29. David Marriot, *On Black Men*, 99.
30. Paul Gilroy, *The Black Atlantic*, 183.
31. Elizabeth Yukins, "The Business of Patriarchy: Black Paternity and Illegitimate Economies in Richard Wright's *The Long Dream*," 747.

longtime affair with another woman. Eventually, as a result of his dealings with local city officials, Tyree is killed, leaving his teenaged son in charge of all of his business affairs. After Fish is arrested for allegedly raping a white woman (a ploy by police to extract incriminating information from him that may get them into trouble), he gets out on bail then leaves the community and his father's legacy and heads for France. Fish's survival and hope lie in his removal from the community that has been denigrated by white men and their collaborations with his crooked father. In an effort to avoid the dishonorable legacy of his deceased father, he moves to a place where he hopes that he can construct an independent identity.

Tyree's most important role is to teach his son how to survive in the hostile world of Mississippi during the 1950s. Fish's lesson begins the day his friend Chris is lynched and his father offers him instructive commentary:

> I been keeping this terrible stuff from you. But I got to tell you what life is for black folks. Tonight you git your first lesson and you got to remember it all your life. Keep your eyes open and learn. This is what you got to live with each day. But I don't want it to keep you from being a man, see? Be a man, son, no matter what happens. (*TLD*, 66)

Tyree impresses upon his son that there is a direct correlation between sex and manhood. While Mr. Tucker offers commentary to his son about the lynching, Mrs. Tucker would rather he not know about the southern taboo, but her husband has the last word on the subject: "He's old enough to die, so he's old enough to know! (*TLD*, 64). Chris's lynching notably marks not only Fish's realization about the dangers black men face, it also affects his opinion about his parents. Fish is stunned and ashamed by his parents' reaction to what has occurred, and his shame regarding their fear succeeds in distancing him from them emotionally. He does not understand the lack of power his parents, especially his larger-than-life father, face in their society.

The narrator implies that the rite of passage for Fish has begun, and the rite involves moving from the protection of his mother to the guidance of his father: "His mother rose and embraced him, taking leave of his childhood, of his innocence" (*TLD*, 64). Fish does not welcome her desire to protect him as the knowledge of Chris's lynching marks Fish's move toward manhood. He consoles her, "'It's alright, Mama,'" he mumbled, struggling for self-possession" (*TLD*, 64). Bassoff observes,

> to acquire his identity, ... , a little boy cannot pattern himself after his mother. At his earliest, he must begin to turn away from her and toward his father; he must begin to make an effort to separate himself imaginatively, or to 'dis-identify,' from the female whom he was once joined . . . and to 'counter-identify' with the male who unto this time has been an 'outsider.'[32]

In this way, Fish is no different from young Richard, who emotionally separates himself from his mother at a young age when she asks him to end her life. However, Fish is able to cling to his father while young Richard is not. Prior to this point, Fish is increasingly "embarrassed" by his mother's "bossing" of the house (*TLD*, 100). He, like the average adolescent, is forging his identity as a man, but in 1950s Mississippi the process is complicated. With his father's help, he will learn how to navigate racially hostile environment while maturing into manhood.

This is the point where Tyree begins to teach his son, as he should, how to treat women; however, Tyree's influence on him is problematic. His father tells him, "Son, your mama's awright, but she's gitting a little odd. It just happens like that with women" (*TLD*, 100). Tyree implies that Emma should be tolerated, at best. Later while Tyree tells Fishbelly how to survive, he also advises him on how to treat women, beginning with Emma: "Arguing with 'em is a waste of time. They just don't understand these things" (*TLD*, 148). Emma is a caricature that exists in the mind of her son with the influence of his adulterous father. Tyree teaches his son that she proves that a woman does not understand things as men do. Trudier Harris accurately describes the chauvinistic perception that Tyree holds: "Instead of trusting her, he views her as a pathetic, church-going buffoon who is more a burden than a wife; the origins of his contempt are not made clear."[33] Tyree's interpretations of the mother's advice to her son serve to negate the religious informed instructions that she imparts. She is and will remain in Fish's eyes "gabbling" (*TLD*, 100).

32. Bassoff, *Between Mothers and Sons*, 52.
33. Trudier Harris, *Exorcising Blackness: Historical and Literary Lynching and Burning Rituals*, 48.

Nearly all of his lessons about manhood are in conflict with women. His first experience with the police marks his personal experience with the southern taboo regarding sex and manhood. Fish's encounter with the police occurs when he and his friend Zeke are arrested for trespassing. The scene is similar to that of Big Boy and his friend's trespass in Wright's short story "Big Boy Leaves Home." Although there is no white lady present at the pond where the boys are arrested, there is one present on the ride to the police station. As a result of Fish's uncontrollable urge to stare at her, a police officer threatens him with castration. Like Big Boy, Fish is treated like a man who desires to be with white women—thought to be every black man's fantasy. As a result of this incident—baptismal through experience—Fish, like Big Boy, loses his innocence: "A clap of white thunder had split his world in two; he was being snatched from his childhood. The white folks treated him like a man, but inside he was crying and quaking like a child" (*TLD,* 113). Fish learns firsthand the lesson that his father wants him to know about the dangers of showing interest in a white woman. Wright reiterates that the mark of manhood in the South is the danger not only of castration and death but clashes with white patriarchy, the system that makes the rules.

When Tyree comes to retrieve him from jail, Fish is "dismayed" by what he perceives as Tyree shamelessly "crawling before white people," and he thinks Tyree "would keep on crawling as long as it paid off." As if Tyree can read his son's mind, he says, "I'll show you how to twist these no-good white folks 'round your little finger'" (*TLD,* 100). Later, Tyree shares his survival secret with his son: "A white man always wants to see a Black man either crying or grinning. I can't cry, ain't no crying type. So I grin and git anything I want" (*TLD,* 149). Fish's arrest brings him closer to his father, who takes him into his confidence. Tyree's strategy is not just to survive, but to manipulate white men to gain some measure of power. Herman Sanders explains that black men have several reactions to the lack of access to social equality. These reactions include laughing it off, playing the clown, resigning, and rebelling.[34] To some degree, Tyree has combined three of these: he admits that he grins; he clearly plays a sort of clown by literally "crawling before white men"; and all of these are his form of rebellion. But through Fish's eyes, we see the dilemma of a man compromising his identity to gain respect.

34. Sanders, *Daddy, We Need You* 4.

In addition to these lessons, Tyree teaches his son that a man must and can have as many women as he wants, even though a black man cannot have a white woman. Tyree's ownership of the brothel allows Fish access to promiscuous, needy women dependant on strong, knowledgeable black men. Tyree encourages Fish to indulge himself in the brothel. There the boy becomes involved with "meat" (his father's term for these women). To satisfy his whetted appetite, Fish becomes involved with the kind of young, illiterate, promiscuous women who frequent Wright's works. Fish meets Gladys, a young "mulatto" who has a biracial, illegitimate child. She fulfills Wright's pattern of uneducated, promiscuous women who depend on men to save them. Furthermore, she is characterized as childish, and Fish finds that "poor little Gladys was just a woman and didn't know. He would take this woman and teach her" (*TLD*, 219). Fish's illogical belief that he can save and teach a peer anything is ironic since he is a high school dropout who lives off his father's income.

Tyree also teaches his son that manipulation of white men—those in power—is the pathway to sustaining oneself economically. With financial stability, no matter how it is attained and maintained, he can better navigate the South. Tyree has achieved this objective through unscrupulous means, which are revealed after The Grove, his club, burns down and many are killed. At that point we find Tyree becomes the "crying type." Tyree, a silent partner in The Grove, faces charges for murder of the forty-two people who are killed in the fire. Tyree has an alternative solution. During the meeting with the chief he has been bribing, "Tyree sat for several seconds, mute, frozen; then he sprang tigerishly forward, sliding to the floor and grabbing hold of the chief's legs . . ." he says,

> "Tell 'em to try a mixed jury, Chief. Just for once, just for me, for poor old Tyree . . ." He lifted his sweaty face and glared at the chief. "You can't let this happen to me," he spoke with almost human dignity. Then as though afraid, he let out a drawn-out moan of a woman with ten children telling her husband that he could *never* leave her. (*TLD*, 263)

After Tyree's performance, the chief resolves that he will speak to the judge about putting blacks on the jury, which would be an unprecedented occurrence. Tyree's decision to attempt to emulate white men by collaborating with them in unethical, immoral, and illegal activities hinders his ability to define himself. Ultimately, he must be the man that they want him to be, but this does not guarantee that he will have access to what they have. Tyree's attempts to empower himself through humiliation problematizes the black masculine identity his son seeks. Tyree is a black man, and he will be reminded of that no matter how much he tries to circumvent barriers set against him because of his race and gender. It becomes obvious that Tyree's need to act "black" for the men only affirms the fact that he is black and, therefore, is relatively powerless in his relationship with these white men. Their ownership of the town as government officials allows them the means to limit who will attain what. Tyree's relationship with them is on their terms and not his.

Notably, Tyree's relationship with these men is not positive for the community. The community here is a space where immoral activities clash with ultra-moral beliefs. More specifically, the female prostitutes juxtapose the religious mother. Tyree appears as a metaphor for Wright's feelings about black communities. Death is pervasive, and it is Tyree who causes deaths and handles the dead. His duality may be compared to Wright's struggle with his father, whom he wanted to know better. The result was that he pitied him but did not hate him. Wright associated the weaknesses of black communities with his father, but he could never abandon his interest in black folks.

Like Wright's, Fish's relationship with his father is complex. Not surprisingly, his interpretation of the scene and his father's dual identity is ambiguous. Earlier he has regarded his father as someone whom he must tolerate: "He unconsciously reasoned in his manner: 'Papa, you are black and you brought me into a world of hostile whites with who you have made a shamefully dishonorable peace. I shall use you, therefore, as a protective shield to fend off that world, I'm right in doing so'" (*TLD*, 169). Fish acknowledges his father's attempt to guide him on a path toward southern black manhood. During the crying scene, Fishbelly is "transfixed":

"Was that his father? It couldn't be. Yet it was . . . There were two Tyrees: one was a Tyree resolved unto death to save himself and yet daring not to act out his resolve; the other was a make-believe Tyree, begging weeping—a Tyree who was a weapon in the hands of the determined Tyree" (*TLD*, 264).

Fish is clearly in a stage where he begins to question his own father's identity. As he does so, he implies that he is unwilling to imitate his father's way of living. Yet, he recognizes the intent behind his father's behavior. Tyree's act of "falling to his knees to beg the white folks for mercy," is an act of survival. On one hand, it is a manipulative attempt to achieve power over the white men, but on the other hand, it is humiliating. He deliberately attempts to control the chief and any other whites who seek to destroy him. Tyree is threatening to whites; for this reason, Tyree's son reluctantly respects him. Ultimately, his eyes become opened to the reality of his father's true identity. Indeed his identity is representative of black men's reality in Mississippi and in America. Fish most certainly realizes, as he did when he noticed the reaction his frightened parents had to Chris's lynching, that a black man of that era will never receive full recognition as a citizen in the South.

Tyree realizes this as well. When his behavior proves ineffective, he implements "plan B": he resolves that he will not be the one to take full responsibility for the deaths. Finally, we understand what motivates Tyree to live a corrupt lifestyle. In an emotional conversation with Mr. McWilliams, he explains his actions: "Niggers ain't got no rights but them they buy" (*TLD*, 290). At the end of Tyree's emotional social commentary, we are told that Fish saw his father for the first time. Fish heard him speak out the "shame and the glory that was theirs, the humiliation and the pride, the desperation and the hope" (*TLD*, 290). Ultimately, black fathers in Wright's fiction, even in *The Long Dream*, often receive very little respect. They are often subjected to white patriarchal racism and thus are forced to survive by making decisions that are not honorable. Fish inherits more than his father's businesses; he inherits the need to form survival strategies.

Forming these techniques take practice, especially when successful navigation of social spaces may mean the difference between life and death. Fish begins learning this as a child. In an earlier scene, he has his first encounter with whites. As he journeys to see his father, Fish is accosted by white males who are shooting dice in the alley. Since one of them considers him, a "crying nigger," to be good luck, they order him to shoot the dice. This scene not only marks Fish's first encounter with white men, it also foreshadows the illegal relations he will have with white men and the "tears" he will shed as a result. More significantly, Fish is forced by the white man to throw the dice; he has no control over his own actions, no choices. He has "luck" according to one of them and is able to make money. The one that makes the money, in turn, gives Fish a dollar. Fish chooses to keep this interaction a secret, even from his father, who will later reveal secret dealings with whites to Fish with the expectation that Fish will "inherit and run the business." Thus, his innocent hands on the white cubes with the "black dots staring at him" undoubtedly symbolize the risk he will eventually take in dealing with the police chief. However, he will reject his father's legacy and leave his father's corrupt model for survival behind. Through Tyree's death and Fish's life, Wright suggests that a son can learn much from his father, but he also has the right to choose what he will accept as part of his identity and what he will reject.

Black Boy is a guide to understanding what motivated Wright's fiction, and for Wright it was a way for him to begin to access and to reconcile his unmet desires regarding his father. Through his autobiography and fictional scenarios, Wright proves that sons may be bound to their fathers by common experiences, but they are separated by their individual choices. His father seems consumed by the southern rural black community where Wright returns in *Black Boy* and the film version of *Native Son*, where he and his father mark the final moment of their separation. Wright's fathers have various relationships with black communities that directly impact their relationships with their sons. Reverend Taylor finds his voice in a black community as his son observes him. Cross Damon abandons his Chicago community to indulge his desire to be independent from his relationships with his sons, mother, wife, lovers, and black male friends. Finally, Tyree is a less-than-perfect father figure, and his problematic relationship with the community inspires, in part, his son to flee it as soon as he can. We can only hope that he has learned from his father's ill-fated life. Wright proves that black men's engagement with black communities contributes a great deal in determining the fate of black men as fathers and as men.

Chapter Three

Malcolm X's Declaration of Independence from His Fathers

The Autobiography of Malcolm X chronicles the life of a black man born in Michigan in 1925, his bout with drugs and a life of crime in various urban black communities, his rise to prominence as the national spokesman for the Nation of Islam (NOI), and his break from that organization to form his own. Though called an autobiography, the title is not accurate, as is well known and is spelled out on the cover with the phrase "as told to Alex Haley." Consequently, the narrative is shrouded in questions about its purpose and authenticity. How should one go about analyzing the narrative? Is it truthful, or is it a version of a truth? And, in terms of its truth, whose truth is it?

The two autobiographies I previously discussed, those by Hughes and Wright, were written by the subjects themselves. And, as I have established, they have a certain purpose. Hughes separates himself from his father and moves toward defining himself, in opposition to his father, as a man with a racial consciousness of himself as a descendant of Africa. Wright sees himself as a southerner in opposition to his family and to any institution he perceives as racist. Unlike his family, especially his father, he will not be "held back," first by the oppressive institution known as Jim Crow and later by U.S. racism in general. The authenticity of their autobiographies is largely controlled by the men themselves with the exception of changes by their editors. Malcolm X was not afforded this luxury.

In his epilogue to *The Autobiography*, Haley attempts to authenticate the narrative as the subject's truth since Malcolm X could not; tragically, he had been killed before its release. Haley began his relationship with the minister in 1960 when he interviewed Malcolm X for a *Reader's Digest* article he was writing on the NOI titled "Mr. Muhammad Speaks." Later, Haley interviewed him for *Playboy* magazine and then proposed a book, noting that by that point "Malcolm X began to warm up to me."[1] To ensure that Haley would indeed record Malcolm X's truth, notes Haley, Minister Malcolm had Haley sign a letter stating, "Nothing can be in this book's manuscript that I didn't say, and nothing can be left out that I want in it" (*TAMX,* 394). By the time the manuscript was ready for review, Malcolm X had broken from the NOI. Haley says that he agonized over Malcolm X's desire to revise the chapters to reflect his feelings about his break from Muhammad, but the minister later recanted. Haley notes that "he never again changed what he originally said" (*TAMX,* 421).

Despite Haley's attempts to authenticate *The Autobiography* as Malcolm X's truth, there has been much speculation by critics about whether an aspiring writer could extract himself from the narrative, leaving only the voice and experiences of the subject, or whether a national spokesperson of an organization and movement could speak honestly about himself. Initially, Malcolm X did not want the text to be written with him as the sole subject. Louis DeCaro sees *The Autobiography* as having been written to "enhance and glorify Elijah Muhammad."[2] Manning Marable agrees but questions the motives of Haley, surmising that Haley was collaborating with the FBI and that his desire in writing *The Autobiography* was to damage the reputation of the NOI.[3] Both Marable and DeCaro note that there are chapters missing from *The Autobiography,* and Marable states further that Haley rewrote lines of the text. What is not made clear, and Marable may expound on this in his upcoming biography of Malcolm X, is what role the editor of the already four hundred-plus pages of *The Autobiography* played regarding any changes or deletions that were made to the text. Stephen Butterfield believes that a comparison of Malcolm X's speeches with *The Autobiography* proves the book is in the voice of the minister and is thus his story.

1. Malcolm X, *The Autobiography of Malcolm X,* with the assistance of Alex Haley, 392, hereinafter cited parenthetically in the text with the abbreviation *TAMX.*
2. Louis A. DeCaro, *On the Side of My People: A Religious Life of Malcolm X,* 4.
3. "The Undiscovered Malcolm X," interview by Manning Marable.

If we go with Butterfield's assertion and focus our attention on Malcolm X's perception of his father and the impact his father's activism had on young Malcolm, which is my major concern here, then Haley's intent is not as important as Malcolm X's presence in the text, which is quite prominent. Talking to others was his livelihood, and it was how he disseminated his evolving philosophy to Haley, who became a historical recorder at an opportune moment. *The Autobiography* shows that Malcolm X had several reasons for wanting to tell his story: "—why am I as I am? To understand that of any person, his whole life, from birth, must be reviewed. All of our experiences fuse into our personality. Everything that ever happened to us is an ingredient" (*TAMX*, 153). He states later that he hopes "if I honestly and fully tell my life's account, read objectively it might prove to be a testimony of some social value" (*TAMX*, 386).

Relying on his "testimony," I will use *The Autobiography*, for I believe it is his authorized biography and the closest we will get to a text that tells his perspective of the events that had the greatest impact on his life, as well as his personal letters, and to a lesser degree, his speeches to discuss how Malcolm X came to define black masculinity for a generation of black Americans and to examine the impact of his father on his identity construction. In the personal oral texts, he reveals his perception of his father, who died when he was six years old, and from that story he also reveals how he defined black masculinity through his observations of his father and other black men, especially his surrogate "divine" father, Elijah Muhammad. What we find is that Malcolm Little/Malcolm X/ El-Hajj Malik El-Shabazz, inspired by his father, saw black masculinity as stemming from both spiritual grounding and political ideologies, which inspired him to join the NOI. Earl Little was a Christian man whom Malcolm X describes as a Baptist minister who used this position to espouse his religious and political ideals to black congregations. Before his untimely death Malcolm X's father provided his son with a political framework, but his son would later advance that thinking by acquiring a spiritual grounding that was rooted in Islam and not in Christianity, for he saw Christianity as a religion contrived by white men that allowed for too many weaknesses in human character. Albert Raboteau defines conversion as being "not just a change in behavior but metanoia, a change of heart, a transformation in consciousness—a radical reorientation of personality, exemplified in the stories of St. Paul the Apostle and the St.

Augustine of Hippo as a life changing event brought about by the direct intervention of God."[4] Malcolm X would come to believe that black men needed a religion that would give them the skills they need to be leaders, both in communities and at home. Ultimately, I argue that *The Autobiography of Malcolm X* reflects his lifelong move toward healing the pain of losing his father but also reflects how he constructed a black male identity that was influenced by his father's strengths as a political organizer and his weaknesses as a Christian.

The Autobiography of Malcolm X uncovers how Malcolm X relied heavily on his perspective of his father to define black masculinity. For the most part, the geographical location of Lansing, Michigan, and its lack of a large black community, at least in the eyes of the young Malcolm, illuminate even further the position of his father in his tight-knit family. In the Little family, the children relied primarily on one another and looked to their father for guidance. In the first chapter of the autobiography, he describes his father, Earl Little, as a proud black man who is not afraid to stand up to white community members. He says, "He was not a frightened Negro, as most then were, and many still are today. My father was a big, six-foot-four, very black man" (*TAMX*, 2). To his son, the Rev. Earl Little is an ideal black hero—a man who loves black folks and advocates for a free black nation. As his son notes proudly, the reverend preached "that freedom, independence and self-respect could never be achieved by the Negro in America, and that therefore the Negro should leave America to the white man and return to his African land of origin"(*TAMX*, 2). Later, this will be the focus of the NOI and an interest of Malcolm X's.

The Autobiography's first chapter successfully shows the significance of other historical and admired, though controversial, black men, specifically Booker T. Washington (1856–1915) and Marcus Garvey (1887–1940). Booker T. Washington, founder and president of Tuskegee Institute in Alabama—an institute of higher education for African Americans—believed exclusively in the idea that black folks could take care of themselves. Even though Washington's name is absent from the narrative, Jamaican-born Marcus Garvey says Washington's teachings influenced him to establish the Universal Negro Improvement Association (UNIA) in the United States in 1916. Garvey espoused a black na-

4. Albert Raboteau, *A Fire in the Bones: Reflections on African-American Religious History*, 152–53.

tionalist ideology by advocating for an independent nation in Africa and encouraging blacks to be independent economically. The infamous leader of the UNIA was a separatist who opposed integration, and his attempts to empower the black masses, like those of Malcolm X and the NOI later, earned him the attention of the FBI, which became intent on dismantling the organization. A black man in power was a threat, which in some ways served to empower him more, but it also set him on a course that would inevitably lead to his downfall. Garvey was imprisoned in 1925, the year of Malcolm Little's birth, for mail fraud and was released but deported back to Jamaica in 1927.

To many, Garvey represented ideal black manhood as he empowered black men and women to be proud of their African heritage and to gain economic strength by investing in black-owned businesses. In a PBS documentary on Garvey, black women interviewees still retained their excitement about Garvey.[5] One said that "he made you feel like you owned one half of the world, and that you didn't own the other half because you didn't want it." Another woman recalls that she heard that when the men marched down the street in their uniforms, white women fainted. For them, Garvey possessed an admirable quality of masculine power, power affirmed by the way he made them as young girls feel and by the way he made white women swoon. While black girls were proud, their counterparts were overwhelmed.

As a child, Malcolm X shared the women's enthusiasm. He states that he was extremely proud of his father's involvement in the Garvey movement. Young Malcolm sees his Garveyite father as "tough," and women encouraged his thinking: "I remember an old lady, grinning and saying to my father, 'You're scaring these white folks to death!'" (*TAMX*, 6). Her observation explained the incident that almost cost the Little family their lives. Minister Malcolm recalls when the Black Legion burned down the family's house because they were not pleased with Little's Garveyism. More specifically they marked him as an "uppity nigger" for wanting to "own a store, for living outside the Lansing Negro district, for spreading unrest and dissention among the good niggers" (*TAMX*, 3). The minister preferred to think of his father as one who was intimidating to whites and perhaps to others as well. In the face of racism, his father was the family's protector—a key role for a black man to play.

5. Marcia Smith, "Marcus Garvey: Look for Me in the Whirlwind."

Malcolm X's descriptions of his father and his father's link to the much-admired, nationally known Garvey allows him to establish himself as a man who is a descendant of other black men who managed, in dire circumstances, to empower themselves against forces that sought to "proscribe their humanity," to paraphrase Richard Wright. Unlike the fathers of Hughes and Wright, Reverend Little is a hero to his son. Malcolm X remarks of his father's death that one of the reasons his father decided to accept the risk and dedicate his life to spreading Garveyism was that he had seen three of his six brothers killed by whites (*TAMX,* 2). Reverend Little would himself later be killed by whites. The minister goes on to establish himself as a legacy of his father's life's work. He states, "I was my father's seventh child" (*TAMX,* 2). According to folklore, the seventh child is special. This statement follows his assertion: "It has always been my belief that I, too, will die by violence. I have done all that I can to be prepared" *(TAMX,* 2). This may seem a prophetic statement considering that he was assassinated before *The Autobiography* could be released, but he says that he has always believed that he would die a tragic death, suggesting here that by nature a black man in the United States will reach a tragic end to his life regardless of the role that he plays in society. But as the seventh son, he feels destined to do more than just wait for death to come; his life must have meaning.

How he defines his meaning emerges from how he perceives his father. Despite his admiration of his father, Minister Malcolm makes clear that the man was not perfect. Reverend Little exhibits behavior that suggests that he preferred light skin. His son believes that it is because he was the lightest child that he was the only one of his father's children chosen to attend the Garvey meetings and was not beaten by his father. He also suggests that his father may have married his mother because her skin was light. She was biracial, the daughter of a black mother and a white father. At the core of their relationship may be the reasoning behind the abuse she suffers at the hands of her big, black husband. While Malcolm says that his father's anger at her may have been the result of Earl Little's jealousy regarding his own lack of education in comparison with her education, the fact that she had lighter skin and despised whites cannot be ignored.

What emerges in this narrative, not unlike in other black men's autobiographies, is the son's critique of the father, which allows the son to step away from his father and to forge his own identity. The first of these for

Malcolm X is while his father has an unstated preference for light skin, his son has a preference for black skin. When describing several of the black people he admires he mentions their dark skin, beginning with his father and including his sister Ella and the wife of Elijah Muhammad. Dark is also synonymous with southern, which makes them more capable of surviving adversity. These darker-skinned people are seen as strong in contrast to whites or lighter-skinned blacks.

Whatever their shade of darkness, black people, even his father, remained vulnerable to racial violence. Malcolm X seems to separate himself from directly expressing any of the feelings that he must have suffered when he learned that his "big black father" had fallen victim to those the reverend had boldly defied. We can only assume that his father's death in 1931, when Malcolm X was only six, left him feeling vulnerable to a racially hostile world, and of course, he was. He focuses more on the impact that his father's absence had on his family, and in particular, how he came to be defined. As his mother struggles to keep her family together despite her own deteriorating mental state, Malcolm becomes increasingly aware of the negative side of what it means to scare white folks. First, the family does not receive the larger of the two life insurance policies Earl Little had purchased. Then his mother is stigmatized as Earl Little's widow and cannot get a steady job to feed her family. Further, young Malcolm is treated with hostility. He observes, "As I began to be recognized more around the town, I started to become aware of the peculiar attitude of white people toward me. I sensed that it had to do with my father" (*TAMX*, 15). This statement reveals the sheer vulnerability that he feels as a young black boy who does not have the protection of his father. His sense of vulnerability is heightened when he overhears adults saying that his father was unable to protect himself from the Black Legion or the Klan and that the Little family had been discriminated against by the insurance company. If these things are true, what can he do to protect himself and his family? It is likely at this point that he begins seeking ways to empower himself.

Eventually, his search for empowerment leads him to Massachusetts into a circle of hustlers—black men who define their life on their own terms. Among those whom he admires are West Indian Archie and Shorty. The presence of Shorty, an older black man, helps the young Malcolm to become acclimated to the streets of Boston and simultaneously helps him to survive his dangerous life as when he provides refuge from West Indian Archie, who wants to kill Malcolm. West Indian Archie himself is a man who has worked to demand the respect of those in "the life." And ultimately, this is what black men want—to be respected as men. Malcolm X does not suggest that these men are in any way surrogate fathers. Their role is to introduce him to practices that help to establish young black men's presences within the community. Such practices allow for a sense of empowerment. Michael Eric Dyson observes, "It was in Boston's Roxbury and New York's Harlem that Malcolm was introduced to the street life of the northern urban poor and working class, gaining crucial insight about the cultural styles, social sufferings, and personal aspirations of everyday black people."[6] Young Malcolm, like Hughes, in the absence of his father actively seeks a place of belonging within a black community. Ultimately, the black community becomes his home.

However, Malcolm's engagement in the culture of the community sends him to another community of black men—a prison—where black men are influential in helping him to change his self-destructive way of thinking. According to Shorty, he and Malcolm X had vowed they would not leave prison as ignorant as they were going in.[7] *The Autobiography* does not, for whatever reasons, make any reference to this. It is clear that the purpose of these chapters is to follow the trajectory of Malcolm's conversion by focusing strictly on his transformation of a man known as Satan to a man who compares himself to Paul, later ordained by Allah to do his bidding with the consent of his chosen divine leader, Elijah Muhammad. We see some inkling that Malcolm Little possessed a consciousness about what would be his purpose in being confined in a criminal institution for seven to ten years. Before his brother Reginald approaches him with the life-altering and self-affirming NOI philosophy, he is having conversations with Bimbi; the older man "fascinated" the twenty-year-old Malcolm Little because he was "the first man I had seen command total respect . . . with his words" (*TAMX*, 157). This, coupled with the fact that a man he admires, in contrast to his childhood teacher who discourages his interest in studying law because of his race, tells him that he is an intelligent person, allows him to perceive his own potential in order to exist outside how he has previously defined him-

6. Michael Eric Dyson, *Making Malcolm: The Myth and Meaning of Malcolm X*, 4.
7. Lisa Zeff, "Malcolm X: A Search for Identity."

self—a man out of control as opposed to a man with self-control. As a result, he begins to take classes to receive an academic, as opposed to a "street," education.

The *Autobiography of Malcolm X* conveys his move toward religious militancy, but it does not at all convey the loving side of the future international leader. In his letters, Malcolm expresses his love for all of his brothers and sisters and says that they are "the only ones in the world I love or have."[8] As he begins accepting Allah his letters are even more lyrical and thoughtful. He tells his "Dear Brother Philbert," "If you could only realize the blissful happiness bestowed upon me by the arrival of your precious letter." He appeared more in tune with communicating his emotions. What is most striking is his attributing his developing relationship with Allah to his mother. It was she, he tells his brother Philbert, who refused the two pigs when "the devil" offered them. Further, he states emphatically that "our achievements arc *Mom's*" (emphasis mine). He goes on to talk about the strong love "among us."[9]

He not only bonds with his brothers, but in prison, too often a prime location for black men, he finds a new father. Malcolm X and Elijah Muhammad have shared the experience of incarceration in the United States. Malcolm X was jailed for burglary and sentenced for dating a white woman, Elijah Muhammad was imprisoned "for encouraging draft resistance" among his followers.[10] Muhammad tells the impressionable Little that they are targeted by the system because of their race. He writes in a letter, "The black prisoner symbolized white society's crime of keeping black men oppressed and deprived and ignorant, and unable to get decent jobs, turning them into criminals" (*TAMX,* 172). Muhammad's act of describing what for Malcolm Little is the "Black man's experience" is significant to a man in need of a role model who can understand his experiences and needs. Muhammad is instrumental in keeping the incarcerated Malcolm Little grounded and stable. Further, the circumstances of Muhammad's imprisonment contrast with Malcolm Little's, making the religious leader look more like a hero to his people. At this point, Malcolm Little desperately needs the attention

8. Malcolm to Philbert, letter, 1948, from Norfolk, Massachusetts, Prison Colony, box 43.
9. Malcolm to "Brother," December 12, 1949.
10. DeCaro, *On the Side,* 26.

Muhammad provides, and as time passes, their relationship develops beyond that of an older man reaching out to a young black man in peril.

The organization that helped to set Malcolm Little on the path from devious criminal to a devoted religious servant, the NOI, has many influences. Noble Drew Ali, formerly Timothy Drew from North Carolina, led a religion-based movement that began in 1913.[11] Ali's Moorish Science Temple of America, like the UNIA, advocated for nationalism and separatism. Specifically, he taught that the religious origin for blacks was "Asiatic" and that blacks were the "Moorish American descendants of the ancient Moabites of the northwest and southwest Africa."[12] Their text was the *Holy Koran*, which was derived from the *The Aquarian Gospel of Jesus the Christ* and "Infinite Wisdom." He taught his converts to refrain from alcohol consumption, extramarital sex, and other immoral behavior.[13] Ali established temples in Chicago, Harlem, and Detroit—the new home of Elijah Poole/Elijah Muhammad. The organization suffered from internal conflicts but not before it had a noticeable impact on W. D. Fard, founder of The Lost Found Nation of Islam, which later became known as the Nation of Islam. Louis A. DeCaro Jr. surmises that "it seems likely [W. D. Fard] was previously involved in Garvey's UNIA and Drew Ali's Moorish Science Temple."[14]

Scholars have found that Fard integrated some of his religious organization's doctrines with Drew Ali's and Garvey's teachings. Fard, whose racial origin is unknown, appeared in Detroit in 1930 as a salesman in the black community.[15] Fard was born in Oregon in 1891, but he claimed that he was a descendant of the Prophet Muhammad and offered an alternative to Christianity. His professed "origins" bolstered his claim that whites were inherently evil and that "blacks were inherently righteous," a teaching that was timely for the newly immigrated working-poor blacks of Detroit.[16] Under Fard's leadership, many of the practices that Malcolm X describes in *The Autobiography*, such as dietary restrictions against pork, premarital or extramarital sex, and abstention of alcohol, were es-

11. Claude Clegg, *An Original Man: The Life and Times of Elijah Muhammad,* 19.
12. Ibid., 22.
13. Ibid., 19.
14. Ibid., 22.
15. Clegg believes that Fard's parents were either Hawaiian or British and Polynesian.
16. Clegg, *Original Man,* 20.

tablished.[17] By 1932, Elijah Muhammad had become Fard's assistant. Fard left the Detroit movement late that year after several arrests. He resurfaced later in Chicago intent on restarting there, but he captured the attention of the local police and reportedly left Chicago in 1934. Before he left, though, he turned the leadership over to his young assistant who believed that Fard was the prophesied divine savior.

Fard's success was rooted in the teaching that made black men into spiritual beings. The NOI's theology had an undeniable appeal to the black poor of Detroit, especially to blacks who could not reconcile perceived weaknesses in Christianity. Many of them had moved to Detroit to escape the violent racism of the South. Further, the fact that Fard was light-skinned and was reportedly of "Asiatic" descent may have made him more credible as one who saw something in blacks that they may not have seen in themselves. His theology then appealed greatly to those who felt they were just as important as whites, but had to conceal their feelings. In sum, Fard taught that the body known as man formed from a single atom that evolved into a black man later named God, or Allah, and that, in turn, the entity created other beings in his own "black" image.[18] To set black men on a pedestal of the highest kind gave black people, black men in particular, a history that they had been previously denied. More important, it gave black men a power regarding determinism about their own futures that could be controlled not by others but rather by simply going back to the origins of their own being as spiritual people. On earth, Fard was the greatest of the spiritual beings who could lead the people out of hell—existence on earth under the regime of racist "devil whites." In Fard's absence, Elijah Muhammad became the messenger to the lost people.

Elijah Muhammad was born Elijah Poole Jr. in Sandersville, Georgia, in 1897.[19] Poole, the sixth son of a Baptist preacher, was called the prophet by his preacher grandfather, likely since his name is that of the Old Testament prophet Elijah. Like Malcolm X, the seventh child of his father, he was thought to have been born to claim a position of leadership. Poole's upbringing in the Jim Crow South was likely the inspiration for his acceptance of NOI's theology. Georgia, also the birthplace of

---

17. DeCaro, *On the Side,* 24.
18. Clegg, *Original Man,* 20.
19. Ibid., 6.

Earl Little, was the location of brutal and random violence toward black men in the form of lynchings and abuses by employers that included physical and verbal abuse and reduced wages. With the hope of escaping the constant threats of violence, he moved with his wife, two children, parents, and siblings to Detroit in the 1920s. During 1931 in the midst of bouts with alcoholism, consistent unemployment, and persistent theological questions, Poole went to a Fard gathering.[20] Under Fard's tutelage, similar in fashion to what he would later offer to Malcolm X, Poole was converted under the name Karriem and became supreme minister of the fledgling organization. Clegg notes of their relationship, "In the final analysis, the relationship between Karriem and Fard was a symbiotic one in which the former gained a much needed sense of self-importance, spiritual enlightenment, and sustenance for a growing family."[21] As Malcolm X would say later about Muhammad, Fard reached out to a man in great need of an identity that would empower him in a hostile and racist world.

This is the black male–centered history that Malcolm X enters and further develops over the course of twelve years, transforming himself in the process. The conversion of Malcolm Little to Malcolm X is much more than a religious experience, even though Malcolm X compares himself to the biblical Paul. It is also a move toward constructing an identity separate from his father's, though he embraces some of his father's beliefs. His acceptance of the NOI necessitates a name change from his father's "slave name" of Little. Within the once close-knit family that depended only on its members, those who join the NOI get closer, but NOI doctrines challenge the family's unity, beginning with the isolation of Reginald when he defies the practices of NOI. The NOI itself in its contrast to Christianity, which was what his father and mother practiced though they may not have been intent on a specific Christian denomination, taught that there was no hell in the afterlife and that white people were devils and that black people were of God. If Malcolm X is intent on casting himself as a man who moves from Christianity to being saved by Allah of Islam, this also means that his spiritual move is tied to his relationship with his father, whom he describes as a man who loves black people but abuses his own black wife. Therefore, to his son, Earl

20. Ibid., 21.
21. Ibid., 25.

Little's racial sensibilities may be honorable, but his Christian spirituality is questionable.

For Malcolm X, the NOI may offer him a way to balance what his father could not. Though Malcolm X would not begin his close relationship with Elijah Muhammad who would become a second father to him until after Malcolm was released from prison, the NOI allowed him to become part of a unified unit, to rekindle his relationship with his own family, and to glimpse what it meant to be part of a family. Upon his release, Malcolm learns from his older brother, Wilfred, the role of a Muslim father and man under the practices of the NOI, which do not differ greatly from the father's role according to the Little family's beliefs. He identifies Wilfred as the "family protector and provider." In this position, he is the first to rise in order to "prepare the way for his family" (*TAMX*, 197). He then performs the morning ablutions, which include giving honor to Allah and following with a ritualistic cleaning. At the family's center is the father. What he experiences as a member of the NOI is not very different from his perspective of his childhood. Clearly, Malcolm X saw his father as the head-of-household, for when he was no longer there, his family structure deteriorated.

At the point that he meets Elijah Muhammad, he carries with him the childhood experience of spending six years with the dominating presence of his father and now he has seen in practice the role of the Muslim man as a father—provider and protector. Yet he has not had a constant and stable model of a man who can offer him the tutelage he desperately seeks. Clegg notes that Muhammad's correspondence with Malcolm while he was in prison was not unusual. Clegg notes further that Muhammad, an ex-convict, had learned from experience that prisons were the best places to recruit converts to the NOI. Malcolm X proves to be an exceptional case, and as a result of his sincerity and dedication to helping to expand the NOI through the recruitment of converts and his ability to appeal to masses of young blacks, Muhammad's interest in Malcolm X develops into a surrogate father-and-son relationship that the young minister cherished. On several occasions in the text Malcolm X remarks about his father-and-son-like relationship with Muhammad almost from the first meeting. He recalls, "As a young minister, I would go to Chicago and see Mr. Elijah Muhammad every time I could get off. . . . I was treated as if I had been one of the sons" of Muhammad and his wife. He also recalls that "Mr. Muhammad had trained me in his home, as if I was his son" (*TAMX,* 257). Their relationship grows as Muhammad trains Minister Malcolm in "worship rituals; the true natures of men and women; the organizational and administrative procedures; the real meanings, the interrelated meanings, uses, of the Bible and Quran" (*TAMX,* 215). As his knowledge grows so does his adoration of his spiritual father. What appears at the heart of their relationship is Muhammad's presence as a model for self-empowerment and racial pride. Further, Muhammad makes Malcolm X a "seen" man. First, he gives him special attention through religious instruction and spiritual guidance. Then, he elevates him and gives him the means by which he becomes a national figure. Muhammad's trust in him advances Malcolm X's faith in the elder man.

Malcolm X's emergence as a leader under Muhammad resulted in his not only gaining a position of power, but also using that position to empower others. His orations are designed to speak *for* black folks as much as to black folks. In a letter that he writes in his capacity as a national spokesperson of the NOI, he affirms his position. The purpose of the letter is to express his outrage about the arrest of "Negroes," including a Muslim minister in Rochester, New York, on February 8, 1963. He conveys his understanding that, according to the people in the community, the indictments were the result of Republicans trying to embarrass Democrats. He writes, "The Negro Community is tired of being used as a political football."[22] Further, as the minister of Muhammad's Mosque Number 7 in New York, he feels such faith in the teachings of Muhammad that he calls himself Muhammad's "wooden dummy" in "an open letter" to Rev. Amos Ryce II he says that as long as he is "sitting in the lap of" Muhammad, "and he is holding me in his arms" that he will be "speaking with a MAN's VOICE . . . yes, I'll speak like a man and act like a man." It is clear, then, that his use of voice affirms his sense of manhood. Elijah Muhammad helps him to access this empowered masculine "self."

Malcolm X's feelings about his spiritual father are the most exposed emotions in the text. The minister credits Muhammad with knowledge that seems unparalleled by that of any other man. Although his description of seeing Muhammad for the first time is based on a memory, the feeling of awe remains. He recalls,

22. Malcolm X to John F. Kennedy, letter, February 16, 1963.

I stared at the great man who had taken the time to write to me when I was a convict whom he knew nothing about. He was the man whom I had been told had spent years of his life in suffering and sacrifice to lead us, the black people, because he loved us so much. And then, hearing his voice, I sat forward, riveted upon his words. (*TAMX*, 200)

Minister Malcolm is clearly mesmerized by the Honorable Elijah Muhammad's presence, but his attachment to him begins with the fact that Muhammad reached out to him. He comes to recognize that his new father was interested in his potential. And he admits, "I worshipped him" (*TAMX*, 204). He later confesses that "my worship of him was so awesome that he was the first man whom I had ever feared—not fear such as a gun, but the fear such as one has of the power of the sun" *(TAMX*, 216). This is a rare moment in *The Autobiography* where his feelings are revealed; in fact, many of the emotions that may be revealed either as feeling or as statement, with the exception of his feelings about his mother, are connected to Elijah Muhammad.

His great admiration for a man whom he "worships," makes his fall from his position as the "son" of Elijah Muhammad, a life-altering occurrence. His ultimate act of independence then, is evident in *The Autobiography* and was evident publicly. When the minister is told by Elijah Muhammad not to talk to the press about the assassination of President Kennedy, he defies this declaration and makes the now-infamous comparison between the assassination and "the chickens coming home to roost." Though he humbles himself later and tells the press that he will submit to the NOI leader's censuring of him on December 4, 1963, for ninety days, one has to wonder why he, while already dealing with tension between himself and Muhammad, would speak to the press. Was it a mere slip of the tongue? Clegg suggests that because of his history of making other, perhaps more controversial statements, Malcolm X did not believe that he would be censured. I would argue that given the fact that he was on shaky ground with Elijah Muhammad regarding discrepancies (namely moral) between Muhammad's teachings and practices along with the fact that he had been growing in this position for twelve years, he was inspired by his desire to be more politically and socially active than the NOI was allowing him to be. At this point, it is clear that he had outgrown the NOI and that his need for independence, though possibly unacknowledged by Malcolm X, may have been apparent to Elijah Muhammad. I would also imagine that the trust that he had in the man that allowed him to believe to some degree that his faults were fulfilling part of Allah's prophecy as Muhammad had intimated left him confused yet hoping for a way that they would overcome this obstacle. He reveals the depths to which he honored Elijah Muhammad: "I guess it would be impossible for anyone ever to realize fully how complete was my belief in Elijah Muhammad. I believed in him not only as a divine leader in the ordinary human sense, but also I believed in him as a divine leader" (*TAMX*, 372). To his great disappointment, he finds that he was wrong.

Malcolm X's "push" from grace was more intense than he lets on in his autobiography. Reportedly, Minister Malcolm's surrogate father was influenced by others who wanted to displace the minister as the national spokesman, and he was most certainly inflamed by his "son's" discovery and investigation of his infidelities with his former female employees. As a result, after their initial meeting where he silences Malcolm for ninety days, Muhammad decides that Malcolm will not be reinstated. After a tense phone call, the minister comes to realize that his relationship with his surrogate father is beyond repair. It is during this conversation that Muhammad reportedly speaks against Malcolm X's involving himself in "family affairs"—likely a reference not only to Minister Malcolm speaking to the women claiming to be the mothers of Muhammad's illegitimate children but also to his relationship with his son Wallace, who was increasingly moving toward Sunni Islam and away from NOI and, simultaneously, his father.[23] Considering how much Malcolm X adored him and how in *The Autobiography* he still states that their separation was caused by the jealousy of other ministers, he must have been devastated by the suggestion that the man he regarded as a second father was now rejecting such a relationship. By their last meeting on January 6, 1964, their amicable relationship was over.

Leaving NOI was a bold emotional step. Despite his treatment of Malcolm X, Muhammad may not have believed that the minister would be bold enough to sever his ties with the organization, and it is likely that he did not want his beloved minister to leave.[24] Malcolm's public break from him led Muhammad to "cry openly in the presence of newsmen."[25] Rod-

23. Clegg, *Original Man*, 206.
24. Ibid.
25. Ibid., 21.

nell P. Collins, the son of Malcolm X's sister Ella and a former member of the NOI, believes that "whatever his faults . . . Elijah Muhammad loved Malcolm X like a son."[26] Despite the growing rift between them, they both appeared to want the relationship to continue. Their correspondence proves the intensity of their father-and-son relationship. In an open telegram to the press dated March 11, 1964, which appears to have been inspired by the tears Muhammad publicly shed upon hearing of Malcolm X's declaration of independence, Malcolm states that he has never criticized Muhummad's family as reported in the press and that he still considers him as his "leader and teacher."[27] He reiterates this point in a letter that he sends to Muhammad on the twenty-first of the month. He also makes clear his reason for his move toward independence as not having simply to do with others trying to separate the two, but also with the lack of movement to "make your program materialize." It would appear that Malcolm X had left his father's home, so to speak, but had hoped that he would not fall out of Muhammad's favor as a result. Their split was, undoubtedly, emotional for both father and son.[28]

Malcolm's decision to leave the NOI left him isolated even from his own brothers, who had introduced him to the NOI. He was labeled a man who was disturbed, a heretic, a charlatan, and most of all, one who needed to be kept away from the other believers lest he infect them with evil. It was these beliefs in NOI and its leader that led Malcolm's brothers to issue warnings to and about him in the press. His brother Philbert X wrote an editorial in the April 10 edition of *Muhammad Speaks* comparing his "brother to Judas and other historical figures."[29] The family that Malcolm had described as close and the brothers for whom he shows admiration in *The Autobiography* are now men on opposing sides with Elijah Muhammad standing between them.[30]

In his moment of isolation, when his brothers under the command of his estranged surrogate father contribute to the negative campaign against

26. Rodnell Collins and A. Peter Bailey, *Seventh Child: A Family Memoir of Malcolm X,* 131.

27. Malcolm X to Honorable Elijah Muhammad, telegram, March 11, 1964.

28. Clegg, *Original Man*

29. Ibid., 218.

30. Haley notes in *Autobiography* that upon Malcolm X's assassination, brother Philbert and Wilfred X stood with Elijah Muhammad at the annual "Savior's Day" celebration the Sunday after their brother's death and affirmed their allegiance to Muhammad (457).

him, Malcolm X extends his hand to other black leaders in the movement. After declaring that he is free of NOI and affirming his belief in Islam, he states, "We must find a common approach, a common solution, to a common problem." The organization opened its membership to "all Negroes [. . .] despite their religious or non-religious beliefs."[31] Though he does not say anything negative about Muhammad, he implies that he had not before made such a gesture because of Muhammad: "Now that I have more flexible approach toward working with others."[32] His willingness to work with blacks of all backgrounds separates him still more from the stance of the NOI, which had a history of mistrusting blacks who were not members of the organization. Collins notes further that the members of the organization "saw themselves as part of a nation within a nation [and] it was probably this concept, more than any other, that distinguished Malcolm and those close to him from members of more traditional civil-rights organizations."[33] His intent to broaden his tactics through inclusiveness of other black leaders was not solely the result of his having been ousted by Muhammad but also a response to criticism of NOI by black people in the community as not "doing anything." His attempt to ally with other organizations is also analogous to his early life. His need to construct an identity as a black man led him to roam the streets of Boston, Detroit, and Harlem with older black men, a brotherhood of sorts. When he left prison, he was accepted into a new black community with a focus on black men led by a "divine" black man. Having broken from that organization, he is in search of another community that he might lead without the direct imposition of another but that works in conjunction with other blacks. The minister does not completely move away from the ideas of the NOI, and we must recall here that with the exception of the Yacub's history, the religious organization's theology with its focus on Black Nationalism was not an NOI invention. Malcolm X's move toward the broader community of blacks from an exclusive organization shows his growth as a leader, which only could have happened outside the control of Muhammad.

Within a year after his break, he establishes the Muslim Mosque and later the Organization of Afro-American Unity. On March 8, 1964, he

31. George Breitman, ed., *By Any Means Necessary: Speeches, Interviews, and Letters by Malcolm X*, 21.

32. Ibid., 20.

33. Collins, *Seventh Child*, 121.

announces the formation of the Muslim Mosque, and four days later, he offers a "Declaration of Independence," his official statement about the organization. It stands as his public move away from Elijah Muhammad. He makes clear that he "did not leave of [his] own free will."[34] During this period, he attributes his break from NOI not to Muhammad but to jealous "brothers" trying to denigrate his reputation. He goes on to clarify his attitude toward independence: "Now that it has happened, I intend to make the most of it."[35] His movement away from Muhammad does not mean that he is against him. In fact, his sister Ella is quoted as saying that "he didn't want to believe anything wrong about the organization to which he had committed his life, and when he did start believing something was wrong, he wanted to put it all on John Ali in Chicago and not Elijah Muhammad himself."[36] At the time of his break he affirms both his religious beliefs of Islam and Black Nationalism: "My religion is Islam. I still believe that Mr. Muhammad's analysis of the problem is the most realistic, and that his solution is the best one."[37] That solution was returning to Africa, and he continued to believe, as had black male nationalists before him, that it would be best, but until that happened black nationalist ideas that focused on black unity, participation in the elections through block voting, and working with other organizations to achieve human rights for blacks were primary. However, he does assert a significant difference between him and Muhammad who has claimed to have knowledge imparted to him by "the divine" Fard: "I do not pretend to be a divine man."[38] For any who may be turned off by the mythology of NOI, Minister Malcolm both rejects the mythology and offers an alternative.

His break from Elijah Muhammad places him in what will be the last phase of his life—discovery. When he makes the Hajj in April 1964, he not only develops spiritually but mentally as well. His stay in Jedda is where his authenticity as a Muslim is determined and where he begins the practice of orthodox Islam. It is there that he learns more about the faults of Elijah Muhammad and grows further in his spiritual journey. In

34. Breitman, *By Any Means,* 19.
35. Ibid., 20.
36. Collins, *Seventh Child,* 12.
37. Breitman, *By Any Means,* 20.
38. Ibid.

this middle space that suffices as a home for him his eyes are opened to the fundamental differences between NOI and Islam, in particular to the essence of Islam. His first lesson is that "Yacub's history" is a contrived mythology that is specific to the beliefs of the Nation of Islam, not Muslims. This revelation also helps him to realize that whites are not inherently evil and out to destroy blacks, as Muhammad teaches. He sees this in practice when a white man, a fellow Muslim, is instrumental in making sure that he gains entry into Mecca. Next he discovers, "In Elijah Muhammad's Nation of Islam, we hadn't prayed in Arabic" nor do they do the proper prostration (*TAMX*, 333). Again, he learns that the man he adored is fallible, even in his religious practices. His knowledge also allows him to revise the beliefs of his childhood that were inspired by his father's conflicts with whites and his own observations of them.

What is most important about his pilgrimage to Mecca is that it both affirms him as a human and gives him the opportunity to see all people as humans. In effect, he experiences humanity on a spiritual level, in contrast to the U.S. experiences that made him feel as though it was "us against them." We may recall here his introduction to NOI by Reginald. His brother's assertion, based on the organization's teachings, that whites are evil is affirmed by his earliest childhood memories of his interactions with whites: Their home is set afire, and he recalls the fire department watching it burn; his father is reportedly killed for "scaring white folks"; his family is divided by the government's social workers; and a white male teacher tells him that he is a "nigger" and therefore cannot be a lawyer. In reference to how he was treated by the welfare workers he remarks, "they had looked at us as numbers and as a case in their book, not as human beings" (*TAMX*, 22). His realization that whites are not inherently evil, that they are not all out to get him as he has believed since he was a child, allows him to develop a sense of reality that revises what his father, Earl Little—through his adversarial relations with some of the local whites—and his spiritual father, Elijah Muhammad—through his letters and teachings—encouraged him to believe. He is able to develop a spiritual identity that is separate from a political identity and that is not steeped in prioritizing man over spirit.

The intent of *The Autobiography* shifts from one that was to enhance the image of Elijah Muhammad and the NOI to one that speaks to the experiences of the speaker, a boy whose father left him in death to a man who was betrayed by another father. It is during this tumultuous year of change in 1964, and after his break from Muhammad, that the minister tries to rewrite the autobiography, which reflects his feelings about Elijah Muhammad, but later reverses this decision when Haley reminds him that he had promised to leave the autobiography as a document in progress. He does, however, change the contract so that the royalties will not go to the NOI but to his own organization, the Muslim Mosque, or to his wife in the event of his death (*TAMX*, 415). Perhaps one of the more revealing moments of his move away from Muhammad is that he convinced two of the women who alleged that Muhammad had fathered their children to file paternity suits against him.[39] Ultimately, he has advanced to a place where his only father is Allah whom he worships not as a member of the NOI but as an orthodox Muslim. As a result, he can begin the process of healing paternal loss (Earl Little) and paternal rejection (Elijah Muhammad).

Islam also influences Malcolm's treatment of women. The father who laid the foundation for his political beliefs and spiritual curiosity also laid the foundation for his feelings about women. Earl Little asserted a strong black masculine presence in his household, in his son's view. Malcolm tried to understand and explain his father's treatment of his wife, Louise. He observes, "An educated woman, I suppose, can't resist the temptation to correct an uneducated man" (*TAMX*, 4). This observation where he seemingly ignores his father's abusive behavior also points to Earl Little's own justification of his behavior. While this may be read as his attempt to assign fault in some way to his mother, it reads more as his unwillingness to overtly critique his father's behavior by casting the blame elsewhere. The only instance in which Malcolm X speaks directly about a flaw in his father's character is when he wonders whether his father favored him because of his light skin. This observation has the effect of making his father a victim of "brainwashing." There is much to read in the subtle.

Notable descriptions of his parents' actions and his reactions show his struggle to speak honestly about his observations and to critique them, such as the above example of his father's hitting an educated woman and another of his mother's whipping him for his illegal activities (e.g., stealing food) after the death of his father. He remarks that what he is most proud of is that he never hit his mother. This statement seems odd

39. Clegg, *An Original Man*.

given that he was a child, but if we relate it back to the father that he admired, it would seem that Minister Malcolm is comparing himself with
his father. He essentially admonishes his father, suggesting that whatever
the reason, his mother should not have been abused by his father. This
is a significant attempt to separate his own masculine Islamic identity
from his father's flawed Christian masculine identity.

His feelings about women and his relationships with them probably
have less to do with what he learned from his fathers and more to do
with his childhood reaction to his mother's illness, although he likely used
what he learned from them to interpret his feelings. Later, he hints that
his mother's mental disability made him feel helpless. At one point he
goes to visit her, and she does not recognize him. He is devastated:

> "The woman who had brought me into the world, and nursed me, ad-
> vised me, and chastised me, and loved me, didn't know me. It was as
> if I was trying to walk up the side of feathers. I looked at her. I lis-
> tened to her 'talk.' But there was nothing I could do" (*TAMX*, 22).

Not only does he feel helpless, but he also has to admit that the role that
he envisions for a black man—that of protector—does not apply here. He
clearly feels vulnerable, and he does not go back to see his mother because
"it could make me a very vicious and dangerous person" (*TAMX*, 22). As
a child, he was helpless to keep his family together, and as a man, he was
helpless to alleviate his mother's suffering from a mental breakdown.

For a black woman to have a mental illness was, in itself, perceived as
a sign of weakness. "She is a strong black woman" is often how black
mothers are described, showing the community's wish to see them in this
light. As an antithetical perspective, a lack of strength would be that she
has shown a weakness, particularly a mental one. Patricia Hill Collins
argues: "Even when they are aware of the poverty and struggles these
women face, many Black men cannot get beyond the powerful control-
ling image of the superstrong black mother in order to see the very real
costs of mothering to Black women."[40] Malcolm X does show a great
deal of compassion and understanding for his mother. Rather than
blame her for the family's demise, he accentuates the role that the state
welfare agents played in dividing the family. He mentions their lack of

40. Patricia Hill Collins, *Black Feminist Thought*, 1.

respect for his mother's refusal of food based on her religious beliefs; he mentions her attempts to bring in another man to the family to help her with her undisciplined sons and to ward off the state; and he describes the discrimination she endured in her attempts to procure a steady income. While she was victimized by the state, which rejected her best efforts, the minister does not deal honestly with the fact that she had a mental defect that may have been exacerbated by the circumstances but was not necessarily caused by the state. He revisits this idea later when he attributes Reginald's mental problems to a "burning" by Allah.

In any case, what he observes and feels allows him to make his mother and her suffering into a metaphor for his life's work. He concludes, "Hence I have no mercy or compassion in me for a society that will crush people, and then penalize them for not being able to stand under the weight" (*TAMX*, 22). Malcolm X admits that his mother was unable to deal with the stress; however, he places the primary blame on society, as controlled by whites, more specifically, the government agency. His childhood experiences with and observations of the system's dismantling of his family and other families as well inspires his interest in those who are of the low-income class. No doubt this contributes to his lack of trust in governments, as it has whites in general. And, the NOI provided a lens for him to feel justified in his mistrust. Of course, as he becomes more prominent, his experiences with the government, especially the federal government, will validate his feelings. In many ways, *The Autobiography* serves to advocate for the people who become powerless under policy structures that hinder when they should help.

What he has learned about women from his father's treatment of his mother is further supported by the ideas of Elijah Muhammad. The NOI teaches that the man of the house must get up earlier than everyone else as part of his duty as a role model. Muhammad also teaches Malcolm X that the woman he chooses to marry should be younger than he. The most striking idea about the role that black men should play in society, especially good Muslim men, is that they must be the protectors of women. Further, in addition to the mandatory meetings of the Muslims on Wednesdays, Fridays, and Sundays, women were also mandated to attend a nursing class on Tuesday nights and a "culture and civilization" class on Thursday nights. They would learn "proper gender relations, child rearing, and household management." In the temples, "Muslim women were placed on pedestals and jealously guarded." They wore long dresses and turbans.[41] Farah Jasmine Griffin observes, "The Nation provides him with a framework that still accepts women's nature as fragile and weak, that also sees women as manipulative, but that encourages men to protect and respect instead of abuse them" (*TAMX*, 218). Malcolm X confirms this: "Now, Islam has very strict laws and teachings about women, the core of them being that the true nature of a man is to be strong, and a woman's true nature is to be weak, and while a man must at all times respect his woman, at the same time he needs to understand that he must control her if she expects to get her respect" (*TAMX*, 230). He then recalls his days as a hustler and his conversations with prostitutes, noting that his experiences with women confirmed what Islam taught.

Influenced by his observations of his parents' relationship, he presents a harsh description of women in *The Autobiography*. Of course, there may be exceptions to this, such as the description of his sister Ella. There is a difference between the women whom he respects and those he does not whom he lumps into one category as women in general. Among the latter would be Sophia, a woman who allows herself to be disrespected by Malcolm Little only to indulge their desires to have a forbidden experience and prostitutes who get paid to manipulate men as a matter of survival. As a result of coming into contact with these women when a teenager and while in search of his own identity as a black man in America with only other black men who are no better off than he, it is little wonder that, with rare exception, he sees them as "flesh."

For the young Malcolm, women served the purpose of affirming his manhood. While in Boston, he struggled to define blackness. For him, middle-class black people were not authentic members of the race as they tried to define themselves according to white societal standards. In his effort to reject "whiteness," he engaged in a brief relationship with Laura, a young black girl who lived with her Christian grandmother. The fact that Laura is black was not enough to satisfy young Malcolm's desire to affirm his blackness. By then, he had conked his hair and purchased a zoot suit. The hairstyle and "hip" suit were statements about the men (though he was a boy) who wore them—that they were part of a culture that affirmed black masculinity for their interest was not in wearing a traditional suit or conforming to any lifestyle that would require one.

41. Clegg, *An Original Man*, 101.

Therefore, as he moved to affirm his black masculine identity by engaging in the street culture of the 1930s, a white woman, and not a black girl, had to be part of the life. Sophia, an affluent young white woman, made him feel as though he had arrived at manhood and at a certain status of black masculinity. Like the suit, Sophia represented his defiance of what was expected or accepted.

From his childhood days to his life with the NOI, Malcolm used skin color as a factor when judging women, a standard he learned from his father and his light-skinned mother. Both men held her accountable for what they perceived as the source of tension in their lives—whites. Minister Malcolm notes that he hates every drop of white blood in his veins. He also exposes the hypocrisy of his father, however, he notes, "I actually believe that as anti-white as my father was, he was subconsciously so afflicted with the white man's brainwashing of Negroes that he declined to favor the light ones" (*TAMX,* 8). Both men embraced half-white or white women, but neither seemed aware of their attraction at the time. Earl Little married a biracial woman and Malcolm Little had a relationship with a white woman whom he could, according to him, control. She proved to be of little importance to him. To be a real black man, one must celebrate blackness and marry a brown woman, as Malcolm did when he married Betty Shabazz.[42] A dark woman like his sister Ella might prove to be a move toward emasculation as he suggests when he describes his sister as being dark and as having been unable to keep a husband.

Despite his varying engagements with women at different phases of his life, there is evidence that his identity changes also included a change in his perception of women. While he paints unflattering pictures of Sophia and other women from his hustler days, he clearly respected his wife. In a letter from prison, he states that he will never marry as to avoid distractions from his work for Allah.[43] Obviously he changed his plans. When he describes meeting and marrying his wife, he begins by noting that his beliefs about women were based on Islam. The core of the teachings contrasted men's strength with women's weaknesses (*TAMX,* 230). He begins the next paragraph, in fact the next line, by stating that he

---

42. Farah Jasmine Griffin, "Ironies of the Saint": Malcolm X, Black Women, and the Price of Protection," 219–20.

43. Malcolm X to "Sister Beatrice," letter, 1952.

had his own personal reasons for believing in this teaching that were based on his experiences with prostitutes. Significantly, this statement prefaces a revelation: "I wouldn't have considered it possible for me to love a woman" (*TAMX*, 230). This is another instance where he separates himself from his emotions and describes his courting of Sister Betty X as one of logical interest. There are no emotions here, but rather an examination of height and age. Yet, when she comes into his presence he leaves the location. His respect for her is probably no more evident in the fact that he does not devote much time to discussing her, thus honoring their privacy. This also suggests his inability to reveal his own emotional weaknesses by discussing his feelings for his wife, the mother of his daughters—future women. According to Betty Shabazz's biographer, Russell J. Rickford, he was a loving, romantic husband who often left little presents in unexpected places in their house for her to find while he was away.[44] Rickford also finds that they had mutual respect for one another.[45] Surely he must have redefined his role as a protector and provider since he was often gone.

Perhaps through his relationship with his wife, whom he says that he trusts and loves, and his view as the father of daughters, he gained a new perspective that forced him to look honestly at the women he earlier had rejected. After describing how he began his relationship with Sophia, which resulted in a blatant rejection of Laura, he makes clear his regret: "One of the shames I have carried for years is that I blame myself for all this. To have treated her as I did for a white woman made the blow doubly heavy" (*TAMX*, 72). Rarely does he critique himself and accept blame for another person's actions and outcome. Notably, his statement reveals a moment of growth when he sees himself as having advanced his idea of what it means to be a black man—one who needs the appearance of a white woman to earn respect among his peers—to a black man who loves black women. His standing as a human rights activist is to uplift the black race and to protect black women. With Laura, he failed but admitting that he was wrong illuminates how this narrative serves as a mechanism for reve-

44. Russell J. Rickford, *Betty Shabazz: A Remarkable Story of Survival and Faith before and after Malcolm X*, 83.
45. Ibid., 86.

lation. Through telling his story, he is given the opportunity to not only examine his life, but to resolve issues that linger.

Confessions to Haley and to the public audience of this personal narrative prove Malcolm X's move toward healing. Admitting his wrongful treatment of black women is not just limited to Laura but extends to his mother as well. By telling his story and learning more about his weaknesses, he becomes strong enough to engage his family about having his mother released from the mental institution where she was housed for most of his life. Haley does not include this in the narrative, but rather leaves it for the epilogue where he is able to provide his own interpretation and perhaps take some credit as well. Haley reports that Malcolm X told him, "I have something to tell you that will surprise you. Ever since we discussed my mother, I've been thinking about her. I suppose that I had blocked her out of my mind." He goes on to admit that he has a habit of shutting things out of his mind when he has a problem that he feels that he cannot solve. *The Autobiography*, as I have discussed above, shows his tendencies to do just that—to avoid what may be difficult to face or may cause the emergence of emotions that make him feel vulnerable. He says, "That's one of the characteristics I don't like about myself" (*TAMX*, 400). Further, he says, "The white man does this" (*TAMX*, 400). His insertion of a comparison between himself and what he perceives to be the consciousness of white men illuminates his desire to be a better black man. He has not completely dismissed white men as not having faults, but his intention is to be, above all else, human. His relationship with his mother, in its complexity, has allowed him to confront his own weakness of consciousness, including his avoidance of love for a woman, and to integrate new characteristics into his idea of black masculinity.

The Autobiography of Malcolm X is a unique "autobiography." It was originally to be a story about Muhammad and the NOI, but it became the story of Malcolm X. His independent voice prevails. Since he did not revise the chapters written before his break with Elijah Muhammad, we can chart the growth of a man as he moves from worshiping and following another man to becoming an independent thinker. Malcolm X was finally able to take the lessons that he learned from his fathers and construct a black masculine identity informed by his relationships with these men as well as his spiritual experiences, personal observations, and relationship with his wife. Clearly, his conversion to Islam and his final move toward orthodox Islam resulted in a transformation regarding his perception of black masculinity. Islam made him see the world, and himself, differently, and it was the critique of the self that gave him the independence to avoid the weaknesses of his black male role models. Islam "is the one religion that erases the race problem from its society," he comments in his letter.[46] Ultimately, this narrative offers an outstanding picture of a man in the process of healing.

46. Open letter from Jedda, Saudi Arabia, 1965. Quotations from speeches and from letters (nn. 8, 9, 22, 27, 43, 46) reprinted with permission of the Estate of Malcolm X. All rights reserved.

Chapter Four

Barack Obama's Dreams

My identity might begin with the fact of my race, but it didn't, couldn't, end there.—Barack Obama, *Dreams from My Father*

The 1960s began with student protests led by four young black men who staged a sit-in at the Woolworth's in Greensboro, North Carolina. Following this, the Student Nonviolent Coordinating Committee (SNCC) was founded. The stories of this generation were bound to change as it moved to transform a nation. A year later, in 1961, Obama was born. Although he could not have known it, young black people were continuing their move to force America to give them equal access, and years later, when Obama became a U.S. senator, he acknowledged that he had reaped the benefits of their success in integrating America. Perhaps as a result of the Civil Rights movement, which included the activism of northern whites, interracial relationships were also on the rise in the 1960s. Obama, born into a changing world, locates himself within the history. He notes,

And it wasn't until 1967—the year I celebrated my sixth birthday and Jimi Hendrix performed at Monterey, three years after Dr. King received the Nobel Peace Prize, a time when America had already begun to weary of black demands for equality, the problem of discrimination presumably solved—that the Supreme Court of the United States would get around to telling the state of Virginia that its ban on interracial marriages violated the Constitution. (*DFMF,* 11)

He suggests that one of the immediate results of the movement was that his father and mother's union became legitimate and accepted by an American institution, though perhaps too late for the son of such a union. Since he was born in 1961, both their marriage and his birth were controversial. For him, his safety was the consequence of having been born in Hawaii and not the South where he thinks that he would have been aborted in a back-alley abortion clinic.

Over thirty years later, challenges to his identity as a "black" man persist. In his response to Obama's *Dreams from My Father,* John Amos contests the label "black" in relation to Obama and replaces it with "biracial." He asserts, "This is not the autobiography of an American man who is black in the historical sense; this is a book by and about a biracial man who had a white Kansan mother and a black Kenyan father, the latter of whom he recalls meeting only once in his life—for a one-month period when he was 10 years old."[1] Amos suggests that Obama's identity as a black man is in question as a result of his father's absence. We may also infer that "black in the traditional sense" has much to do with the fact that neither of his parents emerged from a West African heritage. Amos's assertion that Obama should be labeled biracial recalls the "one-drop" rule of the slavery era. Amos seems intent on overlooking Obama's own desire to see himself as a black man, not only the result of feeling a label imposed on him, as is usually the case with racial designations in the United States, but also out of his desire to understand a racial heritage that was made aloof by his father's absence. Barack Obama's determination that he is an African American is what has led me to include him in *A Fatherless Child.*

Despite Amos's criticism of the author's identity, Obama's autobiography has received critical acclaim. In his review in the *Weekly Standard,* Andrew Ferguson asks, "Once in a while, reading *Dreams,* I stopped to ask myself how it was that such a beautifully exquisitely wrought book could fail readers on its first appearance."[2] Ferguson goes on to deracialize the book by dismissing reviewers and critics who label the autobiography as

1. John Amos, "Black Like Obama: What the Junior Illinois Senator's Appearance on the National Scene Reveals about Race in America, and Where We Should Go from Here," 1.

2. Andrew Ferguson, "The Literary Obama: From Eloquent Memoir to Democratic Boilerplate," 4–5.

"essentially a racial memoir"; Ferguson insists that "Obama's themes are universal."[3] And perhaps they are—relationships between fathers and sons, the promise of America to immigrants, struggles associated with coming-of-age, the struggles of the working class—appeal to all Americans. To believe that they don't would suggest that an African American's experience is not really an American experience; however, the subtitle of the autobiography, *A Story of Race and Inheritance*, and Obama's attention to understanding himself as a black person in America through deliberate interactions with black people, make clear that this autobiography is primarily a "racial memoir." Ferguson's discomfort with the racial marker speaks to the acceptability of the text as American, and not specifically that of a black man's. Obama is Harvard educated, not a criminal, and only flirts with drugs within a certain context. Therefore, his accomplishments meet the requirements of the American Dream scenario.

Obama's racial background and his professional accomplishments as well as how he constructed the text make this work significantly different from the others I have discussed. He admits that he is not quite sure how to classify the text as it may be categorized as an "autobiography, memoir, a family history, or something else."[4] It would seem then that it can be all of the above. The purpose, clearly, is a biracial man's search for his identity as a black American man in the absence of a father who abandoned him when he was so young that he can actually recall meeting his father for the first time at the age of ten. Yet, it is his struggle not just with defining black masculinity that he describes as having occupied the first twenty years of his life but also with determining how to balance that identity with his white American heritage and his unknown Kenyan heritage. In this vein, *Dreams* is complete with extensive details regarding his maternal and paternal family histories, making it significantly different from those of the earlier black male autobiographers, with the exception of Hughes.

It would appear that Obama has succeeded in rewriting the traditional African American men's autobiography where struggle against racism or racially motivated self-hatred is not the focus. What makes his experience common to the earlier black writers is the central theme of

3. Ibid., 4.
4. Barack Obama, *Dreams from My Father*, xvii, hereinafter cited parenthetically in the text with the abbreviation *DFMF*.

Dreams, that is the impact that fatherlessness has on the construction of black masculinity. Obama's revisioning of the black men's autobiography does not mean that a tradition is broken. In fact, it is continued as he poses contemporary questions that bring a new generation of readers firmly into a modern context of defining blackness in the post–Civil Rights era. To be sure, Obama raises questions not only about what it means to be an "African American," but more specifically he shows that the Civil Rights movement, where black men came to public prominence as leaders in their communities, and the Black Power movement, where black men came to prominence by striking fear in whites, left young black men, perhaps those with and without fathers, wondering, "What next?" In sum, he poses the question: What is my role in an increasingly integrated American society?

For Obama, the focus on the "I" as a black subject in a position of oppression shifts, then, to an "I" who struggles to belong. Obama's autobiographical "I," which I will refer to as young Barack or Barack, depending on the subject's age, is critical of himself, his father, and others around him. He begins the autobiography with a preface that establishes what Olney would call multiple selves: first, a retrospective self who has been given credit as a racialized person asked to tell his story because he has "defied the odds and arrived"; second, a self named Barry, the subject of *Dreams* who exists in the somewhat fictional world that Obama, the empowered writer, admittedly creates. This subjective "I" who receives my focus differs from the "I" of Hughes, who sought community among blacks for his goal was to affirm his blackness. On the other hand, Obama's late-twentieth-century search is to be accepted by black Americans while fearing that he will not. Although he, like Hughes, Wright, and Malcolm X, moves to a black community and seeks the company of blacks—notably working-class blacks, as did his predecessors—he realizes that the community has the potential to become the place where he can answer questions about racial identity in America. In essence, he hopes that he will be able, on some level, to learn what it means to live/be black. Clearly Obama cannot pass for white; he describes moments in his childhood when his light brown skin becomes a target of focus by whites. In these instances, he lives as a black person. But he lives largely isolated, for there appears to be no significant community in Hawaii to show him how to navigate the experiences of being black in a white dominated society. In order to rectify this absence of community, Obama moves from place to place, each time increasing the number of blacks he has access to, until he finally makes his *home* in the South Side of Chicago. It is there that he finds the peace that he needs to embrace a black identity and to confront his feelings about his absent father. I argue that the black community becomes a home for the abandoned black son, Obama, to attain healing through racial understanding. Once this occurs, he is free to move forward to confront his feelings about his father in Kenya.

Obama begins his autobiography as the accomplished racialized self who was asked to write his autobiography as a result of having been elected the first African American president of the *Harvard Law Review* in 1990. Accordingly, the book published was not the book he had intended to write when he agreed to the book deal. Ferguson notes,

> He hadn't intended to write a memoir at all. . . . What young Obama hoped to write, instead, he later said, was an abstract, high-altitude examination of American race relations, surveying the uses and limits of civil rights litigation, the meaning of Afro-centrism, and so on, flavored now and then with anecdotes drawn from his own experience as the only son of a white woman from Kansas and a black man from Kenya.[5]

His discussions of the social problems plaguing America as they relate to race and the politics that cease to solve these issues are clear. But the fact that he decided to make those secondary to his own personal need to locate himself as a black man in America and his struggle to do so in the absence of his father speaks volumes about how success—the very success that opened the door to his opportunity to become an American literary writer—cannot be appreciated when questions persist on a personal level. Therefore, Obama succeeds in illuminating how autobiographical writing and its tendency toward self-reflection are key to the achievement of healing.

By the time he published his autobiography, he was writing and publishing in an age that reflected differences in black autobiography. Butterfield notes that autobiographies written by blacks from "1901 to 1961 cover a period of deep alienation and identity crisis," but that since that

---

5. Ferguson, "The Literary Obama," 4.

time, "autobiography no longer moves in a definite direction, with the current of history.[6] However, I would argue that the publication of *The Autobiography of Malcolm X* ushered in concerns that would become common among black men, including an engagement with the black community as a means to define identity and to avoid the alienation that Butterfield references. These autobiographies, among them those written in the 1990s and beginning of the twenty-first century, show an acute internal struggle in which family members are less central to the development of the speaker's psyche than is his understanding of himself in relation to his society, including his peers. Among these works are Obama's autobiography as well as Nathan McCall's *Makes Me Wanna Holler.* McCall, like Obama and Malcolm X, engages in reckless behavior that includes drug use. Malcolm's story became the story of many black men to follow.

Of course, Obama's racial background makes his autobiography different from the aforementioned. His inclusion of family history succeeds in providing the context that led to his questions regarding his father and mother's union as well as its dissolution, resulting in the absence of his father and Obama's lone attempt to locate his identity, now described as a "black American of mixed heritage."[7] Obama is only able to tell the story of his father based on what his grandparents and mother relay to him. Thus, the elder Obama's interactions with his wife and her parents are intertwined with Obama's suspicions about them as white Americans. He begins with his parents' marriage, the details of which are not known to him. In his conveyance of this history, he notes that his grandparents were not in attendance or in support of their union but came around eventually. He feels that "you had to listen carefully to recognize the subtle hierarchies and unspoken codes that had policed their early lives" (*DFMF,* 13). Why they were not supportive, he suspects, has much to do with their own backgrounds.

Obama had two dilemmas: he had to construct a male identity, and he had to construct a racial identity. I do not suggest here that the two must be formed exclusively or interactively. Hughes's idea of masculinity is related to his earlier memories of his father. We may recall Hughes's

6. Butterfield, *Black Autobiography,* 93.
7. Barack Obama, *The Audacity of Hope: Thoughts on Reclaiming the American Dream,* 10.

pleasant memory of his father's saving him during the earthquake and his fantasy of him as a John Wayne–type hero moving about in Mexico on horseback. Hughes seeks a hero, a protector. Ultimately, black masculinity as his father would have determined it is measured by a man's ability to make money and to keep it. This is where he and his son part terms. Wright appears to think of a man more in relation to his acceptance of responsibility to his wife and children. Malcolm X saw a black man in terms of how he struck the fear in white men by "telling them the truth about themselves." These black men may not have had long and sustaining relationships with their fathers, but the contact they did have allowed them the time to process how they felt about their fathers' representation of themselves as black men. Obama's father left him too early for the boy to have any memories of the man. Consequently, he was introduced to masculinity by his observations of other men—his Indonesian stepfather and his white grandfather—before he had much exposure, which he has to actively seek, to black American culture and collective experiences.

Between the ages of six and ten, Obama lived in Indonesia with his stepfather. Not until his move to Indonesia did he find himself confronting his blackness, though he had noticed by the time he was six years old that there was a difference between him and his family. When he asked about this and what response he was given by his family is not provided. The first instance of his confrontation with blackness was when he perused a *Life Magazine* in the library in Indonesia and discovered a story about a black man who engaged in a procedure that turned his skin white. The young Barack was confused and surprised that any black person would desire such an existence. Though he was unclear about the man's motivation, what was clear was that he did not know the history that would lead a black person to undergo such a controversial procedure. In Hawaii, he had been shielded from the reality of racial prejudice, the same racial prejudice that his estranged father no doubt experienced.

Young Barack was an "other" in Indonesia, and he had to rely on his stepfather for guidance. Lolo, his stepfather, became his earliest model for a father and a man. Though his mother would eventually divorce her Indonesian husband, Obama describes him in the book with respect and fondness. His stepfather was the first and only consistent father that young Barack has. His need of a father figure was exacerbated by the fact that he was in a land where he was among the minority, a foreigner, and an outsider. And, though his mother possessed such a status as well and they surely both looked to Lolo to help them navigate their new environment, young Barack recalls his natural desire to connect with a man who could parent him in ways that his mother could not. Lolo introduces him as his son. Lolo's acceptance of his stepson offers the young Barack a sense of belonging that may take the place, on some level, of the paternal abandonment he is processing. The relationship he describes with Lolo speaks to the need of belonging and the fear of rejection that his father's abandonment caused and that is the root of inspiration for *Dreams from My Father*. Throughout the book, his social status in Indonesia and his attempts to fit in with the other children in the area are mirrored later in every instance where he is in a new location in search for a communal experience—in high school, Occidental, Chicago's South Side, and Kenya.

Young Barack credits Lolo with giving him his first lessons in manhood. In his childhood, it was Lolo to whom he turned "for guidance and instruction" (*DFMF*, 38). Obama describes him as a solemn, introspective, and quiet man with a cynical disposition toward the life that he lives in Indonesia. Lolo had been a student in America, where he met and married Obama's mother, but had been abruptly recalled to Indonesia to serve as a soldier during war. He talked with his young stepson about preserving his money and not giving it to every beggar. To do so was to have a soft heart like a woman: "you will be a man someday, and a man needs to have more sense" (*DFMF*, 39). He recalls this advice while Lolo is teaching him how to defend himself from would-be aggressors. Obama shows admiration for Lolo's detachment from young Barack where he offers "matter-of-fact" advice, leaving him to interpret Lolo's distance as "imply[ing] a manly trust" (*DFMF*, 38). Further, he gives lessons where politics and manhood are comparable: "Men take advantage of weakness in other men. They're just like countries in that way" (*DFMF*, 40). In this way, he imparted the importance of strength. Lolo eventually died from alcoholism, but it is clear that he made a major impact on the boy Barack.

His consistent male role model was his maternal grandfather, whom he called Gramps. Obama does not say much about the kind of man his grandfather was, he resists this and relies more on providing facts about his background and leaving descriptions of scenes to the reader for interpretation. His grandfather loved women and adventure, according to his critics and the oral legend that Obama inherited, but he was more a broken man by the time Barack came of age. Obama recalls his grandfather struggling to make money as an insurance salesman. Obama's interpretation of his grandfather's attempts to sell insurance to people who were largely uninterested speaks to his view of him as a man. He would observe "the desperation creeping out of his voice" while Gramps tried to make appointments, a "stretch of silence," and if he was successful "the pain would pass" (*DFMF*, 55). His grandfather's attempts at success in this role contrasted with his grandmother's success as a bank executive. She had been an industrious woman who, without a college education, rose from secretary to the first vice president of a local bank. Her promotion meant that she made more money than her husband, which was, according to Obama, in the era of the 1970s a source of contention between the two.

Before he was a teenager young Barack accompanied his grandfather to places where his grandfather was in the minority as a white man but seemed oblivious to the meaning of his presence in these places. One such place appears in an incident Obama recounts. He and his grandfather visit a bar in the red-light district, a visit that is to be kept secret from his grandmother. It may not be his visit to the bar itself that he wants to keep a secret from his wife, as much as it is the location of the bar where "hard-faced, soft-bodied streetwalkers" are present (*DFMF*, 77). Once inside, young Barack looks at "pornographic art on the walls" and observes the men at the bar as well as his grandfather drinking scotch while the youngster engages in a conversation with another frequent patron. With this scene, whether true or not, Obama joins the ranks of earlier black men autobiographers Wright and Malcolm X, who visit bars during their childhood and who also have the experience of feeling welcomed by a community of people who do not question their presence there. However, these earlier writers were not taken there by their white grandfathers. It would appear that Gramps is seeking a place where he can feel welcomed and where his grandson can feel as though he is having an experience that is not completely *whitened* by the everyday experiences of going to the predominantly white prestigious school that he attends and then going home to live with his white grandparents.

Gramps also takes the young Barack with him when he plays cards with the older black men, again exposing him to a black male experience. How conscious Gramps was of these acts we will never know. But

what is clear is that his grandson was conscious of them and had diffi-
culty processing these moments. Black men may be present at the card
games and at the bar, but since his grandfather is at the forefront of these
memories and the other, nonwhite men are in the background, what is
he supposed to learn about the ways of men? That in order to be men,
they must often remain isolated from the women who love them? He
thinks, "What my grandfather sought there was the company of people
who could help him forget his own troubles, people who he believed
would not judge him" (*DFMF,* 80). What, exactly, does he not want
judged?

His grandfather's presence in the bar and at the card games speaks to
teenaged Barack's budding sensibilities about what it means to be white
in America, which seems to surface before his questions about what it
means to be black. He notes that though he is young he "had already
begun to sense that most of the people in the bar weren't there out of
choice" (*DFMF,* 78). He strongly suggests here that he realizes, without
being told, that his grandfather has a privilege that they do not. For whatever their circumstances are in life, many of the people there have no
middle-class lifestyle to return to the next morning. His suspicions about
his grandfather's presence are confirmed when he seeks Frank's opinion
about his grandmother's fear of black men. Frank, a black man, responds
that his grandfather can come to his house and fall asleep on his chair,
but that Frank cannot do the same at his house. By this time, Barack—
known as "Barry" in order to distinguish him from his father—is a
teenager and he has begun his attempt to define himself as a black man;
he has also certainly come to realize that his grandfather cannot help
him to achieve a racial identity. However, his grandfather's presence allows him to see when he is young that there is a difference between black
men and white men. Barack's questions collide with Frank's life experiences and, in the process, provide a catalyst for him to begin to think
honestly about the differences between black and white and how these
differences impact his position in society.

Barack seeks to understand the white perspective through Frank. What
surfaces prominently in *Dreams* is Barack's questioning of his grandparents' sincerity about African Americans. Since autobiographies are a
kind of overlapping introspection of events that have already occurred,
we come to understand what motivates his questions. The most remarkable of these is his grandmother's interaction with a man at a bus

stop that frightens her so much that she is unwilling to return. She and her husband argue, and it is not until Barack tries to intervene that he learns that the man whom she fears is a black man. He wonders then how she perceives him as a black man. In this instance, he concludes that even though he does not doubt their love of him, "I knew that men who could have easily have been my brothers still inspire their rawest fears" (*DFMF*, 89).

His grandparents' dealings with race surface in the stories they tell about Barack Obama Sr. The senior Obama had been admitted to the University of Hawaii from Kenya after he wrote to universities asking for a chance to prove himself. He left behind a young wife and their son, Roy, and daughter, Auma, to begin his studies at the university in 1959. He was then twenty-three and the first African student to attend that university. In a Russian language course he met Ann, whom he eventually married. When Obama Jr. was two years old his father left Hawaii to study at Harvard, and he eventually moved back to Kenya to work in the government. He died there in a car accident. These are facts that Obama was able to cobble together after talking with various family members on both sides of his family, but when he was a child, his grandparents' stories set the foundation for whatever image he had of his father. He retells the stories. The first is one of his grandfather's about his father lifting another African man off the ground for accidentally dropping his father's pipe over a ledge. After this story, Obama inserts: "[My mother] preferred a gentler portrait of my father" (*DFMF*, 8). She challenges her father's assertion that her ex-husband actually lifted the man off the ground and over the ledge. At the core of this dispute is the image of a barbarian black man prone to illogical anger.

His father as an overtly racialized figure does not factor into these stories with one exception. His grandfather witnessed a man call his father a nigger in a bar. While Gramps sits quietly, Obama Sr. walks up to the man "smiled, and proceeded to lecture him about the folly of bigotry, the promise of the American dream, and the universal rights of man" (*DFMF*, 11). Obama says that he was skeptical about the "truthiness" of this particular story, and the memories of the people telling the stories, but it was authenticated years later by a man who had witnessed it. For him, the stories do not help him learn more about his father, probably because they are too puffed up, and he questions the ability of a white man to tell the story of his black father. He asserts, "They said less about the man himself than about the changes that had taken place in the people around him, the halting process by which my grandparents' racial attitudes changed" (*DFMF,* 25). Yet, if we are to believe that the story is true, it exhibits much about his father's character, namely his ability to talk to others, even racists, and successfully make them confront their own weaknesses. He was as successful at doing this with the man in the bar as he was at convincing his father- and mother-in-law to accept him as their daughter's husband. These stories have the affect of making his father an icon for the kind of success that his son will later strive to attain.

Through these stories and his mother's attempt to locate her son within black American occurrences, Obama sees himself as black and begins to have some idea of what that may mean. In Indonesia, his mother introduced him to the Civil Rights movement. Obama was not in the United States during this emergence of young black men as visible national leaders, and his mother, though relocated in Indonesia, strove to make her son feel connected to blackness in a variety of ways. From his mother he learned about racism in the southern schools and the fight to gain rights for blacks: "She would come home with books on the civil rights movement, the recordings of Mahalia Jackson, the speeches of Dr. King" (*DFMF,* 50). His mother's musings about children learning from hand-me-down textbooks motivated him to become a diligent student. These lessons also motivate him to have pride in a black identity: "To be black was to be the beneficiary of great inheritance, a special destiny, glorious burdens that only we are strong enough to bear" (*DFMF,* 51). Obama constructs his mother as a woman who, though white, encourages him to embrace a black identity by providing him with stories, but she cannot guide him in how to translate those stories into his own individualized identity.

Knowing about the struggles of black people and their accomplishments does not alleviate the black boy's confusion about his identity. Living in the United States where he must live as a racialized citizen forces him to find out what that means. In *Dreams'* sequence, it is not long after he returns to the United States from Indonesia that he meets his father for the first time. The adults appear oblivious to the ten-year-old Barack's fears and distrust of the visit's meaning. What does become clear is that his classmates will see him as different from them, and he had hoped to not be seen as such. He describes the experience of being teased for liking an African American female classmate, Coretta. The young Barack reacts by pushing the girl away, and the act exhibits a shunning away of a black identity to appease white peers. Next, in this sequence is his father's introduction that causes him to begin to think favorably about his personal history with blackness.

Barack Obama Sr.'s visit is emotional for his son as revealed by the resurfacing of his fears regarding paternal abandonment. Prior to his coming it becomes clear that young Barack knows nothing about his Kenyan history as evidenced by the story he tells his classmates. He constructs a history that casts him as an heir to a tribe of feuding warriors (*DFMF,* 63). His own investigation of the history of the Luo uncovers a library book that leaves him feeling disappointed by the images of the "primitive" people the book portrays. He learns that they raise cattle, live in mud huts, and wear thongs (*DFMF,* 64). Interestingly enough, though he had questioned earlier the *Life* magazine article he uncovered in Indonesia, he does not question the legitimacy of the article he reads in the library nor does he seek another source. This article introduces him to the problem with how African nations have been portrayed in Western societies. As a result, he is further alienated from the African identity that his father was not present to help develop.

His father's visit interrupts the images that have emerged from his family's stories about his father. Young Barack faces a man who is "skinnier" than he expected, not someone who appears strong enough to lift a man off the ground; Barack even describes him as "fragile." Eventually, the conflicts that have piqued his interest about his father and his grandparents' feelings about him surface. Barack has not confronted his father about his having left for Harvard and not returning, but now he notes that "after a few weeks he could feel the tension around [him] beginning to build" (*DFMF,* 67). Barack's anger erupts when his father tries to parent him by forbidding him to watch television and telling him to do more work; young Barack does not have to guess that resentment exists. The tension appears to be between his grandparents and his mother, who has decided to have a relationship with his father. He says, "I listened to my mother tell her parents that nothing ever changed with them" (*DFMF,* 68).

Despite Barack's confusion about where he is located as the son of a man whom his grandparents seem to tolerate at best, Obama Sr.'s brief visit gives him a glimpse into what it means to belong based on a history. His father gives a talk at the school, speaking about the Luo in particular and Kenyan history in general, and young Barack's teachers "beam with pride" and express the view that his father is "pretty impressive." His classmates ask questions and one child who asks about "cannibalism" later tells him that his dad is "pretty cool" (*DFMF,* 70). Most of all, Coretta had an "intent look," and her expression was one of "simple satisfaction" (*DFMF,* 70). From his father he learns about the history that a book could not give him. He also learns the importance of voice, more specifically, how using the voice to provide knowledge can empower not only the listener but the speaker. Barack utilizes the gift of this lesson by retelling the moment in the form of autobiography.

Despite this memorable event, it appears that his father was there not long enough for father and son to bond but for Barack to develop more a need to bond. In essence, his father's month-long visit unleashes a variety of emotions that the boy cannot process. From these emotions emerge questions: When his father admonishes him for watching television instead of studying, is the child's anger the result of his feelings of abandonment or the typical anger of a child wanting his way? His father's visit to the school makes him fearful. Is it the embarrassment of a son who fears that his father will make him appear "uncool" to his peers, or is it the result of mistrust of the father he does not know? Or, does he perceive his father's presence as an invasion of his home space? In one paragraph, Obama crams in a litany of broken narrative memories that all involve young Barack trying to emulate his father's behavior, including his clapping when his father does at a concert and holding a book as his father holds his. If these acts do not betray his feelings about his growing attachment to his father and his attempt to know him better, his concluding sentiment does: "When I mimic his gestures or turns of phrase, I know neither their origins nor their consequences, can't show how they play out over time. But I grow accustomed to his company" (*DFMF,* 71). On the day of his departure, Obama Sr. gives his son dancing lessons to the "sounds of your continent" (*DFMF,* 71). It is to that continent that his father returns, leaving behind a son who must construct his identity with these scraps of memories.

Young Barack has met his father, seen him, and heard his voice, but he does not know why his father does not stay in the United States to parent him. Not until he is older, according to *Dreams,* does he learn the truth about his parents' separation. *Dreams* consists of his searching for the answers that were not given to him when he was a child, either because the questions raised emotionally charged issues or because he was reluctant to ask questions, fearful of what he might learn. He relays that when he was in his twenties his mother told him that her parents had not been supportive of the marriage but had relented. However, Obama's grandfather in Kenya wrote her father a letter forbidding the marriage because he did not want "the Obama blood sullied by a white woman" (*DFMF,* 126). When he travels to Kenya he learns that his grandfather was following traditional customs by insisting that the elders come to a meeting of the minds about their children's marriage. What is not sufficiently addressed is the fact that Obama Sr. was still married, by custom, to his first wife, Kezia. His father's inability to sustain a relationship with his wives or his children is clear in the fractured stories Barack hears. Barack struggles to piece together a coherent image of his father based on what he knows from the month he spent with him and what he absorbs from others.

In contrast to his demanding father is his gentle mother who, when she appears in the narrative, acts as a constant intervener. After his father's death we receive two more perspectives about the visit. His mother informs Barack that his father had asked her to return with him to Kenya, but she could not because she was still married to Lolo. She also tells him that the divorce was her idea and asks him not to blame his father for the man's absence in their lives. Upon hearing the news of Obama Sr.'s death, she reveals why she remained seemingly faithful to her first marriage and remained hopeful about her ex-husband and her son's relationship. According to Obama, "She saw my father as everyone hopes at least one other person might see him; she had tried to help the child who never knew him see him in the same way" (*DFMF,* 127). He ends this interpretation of his father and mother's relationship and assessment of his mother's feelings for his father by stating that when he called his mother to tell her that his father had died, he heard "her cry out over the distance" (*DFMF,* 127).

While his mother is present, except for the time she is in Indonesia, she cannot help him to develop an understanding of black culture and life; therefore, he is left alone to determine his identity. During his teen years he begins to search for his own black identity. His search includes forming relationships with other young black men who provide him with a model of blackness. First, there is his friend Ray, a fellow black male student from Los Angeles at Punahou to whom the teenaged Barack looks for help forming a black identity. Though his father has been writing to him from

Kenya, he appears to have no consistent black male role models with whom he can converse; therefore, he welcomes Ray as his peer. Obama describes him as having "a warmth and brash humor" (*DFMF,* 72). Ray appears as a kind of trickster figure, almost a caricature of the black man whom Obama would like to be or at least the kind that he thinks is an "authentic" black man in America.[8] By this time, he has already determined that he "need[s] a race" (*DFMF,* 27), and Obama admits, to some degree that Ray is a bridge to black adolescent experiences: "Through him I would find out about the black parties that were happening at the university or out on the army bases, counting on him to ease my passage through unfamiliar terrain" (*DFMF,* 73). Obama has not been engaged in a black community, but a representative of the black community comes to him and offers him conversations about race and racism.

Barack's relationship with Ray sets up an angry tug-of-war between understanding of himself through others and a need to belong to a community that is aloof. At times, their conversations seem to follow the pattern of Ray posing a problem and Barack questioning the existence of the problem. The first conversation presented involves Ray stating that young women are not interested in dating him because of the color of his skin. Barack poses other possible reasons why this may not be the case, concluding that it is harder for them to get dates because there are so few black girls, but "that don't make the girls that are here racists" (*DFMF,* 74). Mostly, their blackness, as is often the case, is seen through contrast and conflicts. One of Barack's angrier moments is a blatant confrontation with race where their white friends are so uncomfortable at a party of mostly black guests that they insist on leaving early. The fact that they admit to Barack that their brief experience as minorities has made them sympathize with the experiences he and Ray have every day only makes him angrier. Without realizing it, they have revealed an unspoken power that they possess as whites. While they can choose to return to the safety of their lives in the majority without thinking much more about the incident, the conflicts that he is dealing with regarding race will follow him for years to come, at least, we know, until he writes about the racial conflict.

Perhaps this lack of an older black role model is what made him begin piecing together certain practices that might be typical or expected of

8. His 1979 yearbook refers to Ray. Steve Dougherty, *Hopes and Dreams: The Story of Barack Obama* (New York: Black Dog and Leventhal, 2007) 50–51.

black men. He admits, "I was living out a caricature of black male adolescence, itself a caricature of swaggering American manhood" (*DFMF,* 79). From black athletes he learned how to exhibit an "attitude" that was about the individual earning respect, irrespective of who his father was. He also learned how to intimidate an opponent and to keep feelings of vulnerability—"hurt or fear"—hidden. What he learned on the court, he suggests in the next few paragraphs, also helped him to confront any social opponent, particularly any who appeared racist. This included the white coach who "jokingly" warned Barack that touching a piece of paper might result in his color rubbing off on it. In *Dreams,* he recalls other lessons in forming and exhibiting a black male attitude that focused on conversations about "white folks" and what they were likely to do or had done to blacks. All of these practices, he implies, are tied to the possession of a rage typical of young black males. He remarks, "Our rage at the white world needed no object" (*DFMF,* 81). His shift from "I" to "Our" gives him a sense of belonging, allowing him to feel understood and part of an experience that is uniquely that of African American males, as he defines it.

The source of his racial rage is not clear. Is it the result of a rite of passage for anyone claiming to be black, or is it merely what he perceives as a black identity? His questioning of Ray's "judgment" regarding his friend's reading of race persists to the point where Barack wonders about Ray's "sincerity" (*DFMF,* 81). In the construction of their relationship, Obama seems to conclude that authenticity is up to the individual to judge on his own about himself. He states, "You couldn't even be sure that everything you had assumed to be an expression of your black, unfettered self—the humor, the song, the behind-the-back pass—had been freely chosen by you." Consequently, the result was to withdraw and to recognize that "being black meant only the knowledge of your own powerlessness, of your own defeat" (*DFMF,* 85). His use of "you" separates him from the "I" and projects an unidentified self that has yet to understand the individual speaker or the communal "our." "Your/you" speaks more of a powerless subject, separated from the empowered "our/we." It is precisely the feeling of "powerlessness" that motivates much of his perception of blackness, and he must find a way to combat this powerlessness without succumbing to stigma.

Black male adolescent anger and its relationship to the search for identity in America is not exclusively Obama's. Like Hughes, Wright, and

Malcolm X, Obama looks toward books to help him to find his own voice and, in many ways, to authenticate his own experience as he attempts to locate himself socially and historically. Hughes begins *The Big Sea* by throwing books off the ship bound for Africa. He returns to America and eventually becomes part of the artistic movement known as the New Negro or Harlem Renaissance movement, and he speaks of older writers, among them Du Bois. Elsewhere he says that Paul Laurence Dunbar inspired his use of black dialect. Richard Wright speaks largely of H. L. Mencken's ability to use words as weapons, but scholars such as Robert Stepto link his autobiographical style with that of Frederick Douglass. Malcolm X lists a number of writers whom he read in prison, including Du Bois and Carter G. Woodson. Obama sees these men as having withdrawn, embittered and exhausted by/from American racism, as Herman Sanders asserts. What hope, then, is there for black men pondering similar dilemmas in the late twentieth century?

Although Obama links himself literarily and racially with these earlier black male writers, he differs greatly from them in significant ways. First of all, their identities as black people are not questioned. Simply put, their relationship with other black communities does not force them, as it does Obama, to explain themselves to other blacks or to feel challenged by trying to belong with them. In this way, they possess a power that Obama does not have. Obama's power struggle—the power to define oneself as a black individual in relation to an idea of universal blackness—is best shown by Zora Neale Hurston in *Their Eyes Were Watching God*. Not until Janie sees herself in a photograph does she realize that she is black or different from the other children. (We might consider the young Barack's reaction to the visual image of the black man turned white in *Life* magazine.) To her, she is Janie, but until she meets Tea Cake, she is what everyone else says she is. Nanny says she should be a wife. Logan says she should be his obedient wife, as was his previous wife. Joe says she should not converse with the community and remain near him. Tea Cake allows her to be Janie, part of a black community. Barack is treated as though he is black/different by his peers, but he has no idea what black means other than being different. Achieving understanding of blackness by becoming part of a black community occurs deliberately. He does this incrementally as life stages allow, first through forming a relationship with a black male friend, then by observing other black males, and later by examining other black men's writing.

The second significant difference between him and these writers is that he is biracial while they are black. Barack looks to Hughes, Wright, and Malcolm X to help him better understand what it means to be black, noting that Malcolm X resonates more clearly to him than the others since his mother was biracial. As such, his acknowledgment of Du Bois's idea of the double-consciousness as an experience that is an inherent part of all African Americans' experience of being both Americans and people of African descent at the same time has an added piece when he tries to balance that understanding with whiteness. His struggle with being both black and white exacerbates his fears relating to where he belongs: "The constant, crippling fear that I didn't belong somehow, that unless I dodged and hid and pretended to be something I wasn't I would forever remain an outsider, with the rest of the world, black and white, always standing in judgment" (*DFMF,* 111).

His interest in Malcolm X does not resonate with his peers, one of whom tells him that he does not need books to "tell [him] how to be black" (*DFMF,* 87). Their difference is highlighted not only through Ray's foolish proclamation, but also through Barack's need for the books of black men to at least show him in which direction he should look.

He has not spoken much about what it would mean to be white, instead focusing on how whites treat him or may potentially think about him, but there is an unstated concern with the meaning of whiteness. Unstated and avoided, perhaps, because of what he observes about whites and what he hears is the relationship between whites and blacks. Is white bad? His white grandfather assumed privilege among people of color without consideration; his grandmother showed fear of black men; his white "friends" were uncomfortable around him and other blacks. In the face of these personal experiences and the underlying racial history, Barack's search among black male letters to define whiteness gives him a glimpse of hope that his predicament may not be dire. It is Malcolm whom he sees as having a perspective different from the black American male's experience. Malcolm X's assertion that he regretted the white blood in his veins made him think more of Malcolm X's move toward "self-creation" and "self-respect," particularly as these ideas relate to his rejection of the Nation of Islam teaching that whites are inherently evil. Malcolm X's revelation speaks to the maturing Barack about the possibility of "eventual reconciliation, that hope appeared in a distant future" (*DFMF,* 87). In this way, his black and white selves could peacefully merge, as Du Bois says, to make oneself. Or, perhaps, he, a son of both black and white, could be a model for reconciliation between the races.

Obama next discusses his years in college. From books to an academic black community in Los Angeles, he continues his need to understand blackness so that he can firmly belong to the race. At Occidental College, he connects with young would-be campus activists from various backgrounds. This is the section of Obama's autobiography that has received the most attention from conservatives, who focus on his early college years and the reckless lifestyle he describes. The impact of his father's absence emerges when he is a college student. Obama introduces his teenaged, college self as high and argumentative, admitting, "I had learned not to care" (*DFMF,* 93). He indulges coping mechanisms: "Pot had helped, and booze; maybe a little blow when you could afford it. Not smack though" (*DFMF,* 93). In retrospect, he sees himself—relying on the self-avoiding "you"—as heading toward an addiction that had little to do with wanting to be seen as a "down brother." This was his way of trying to avoid probing his identity.

Getting high was Barack's way of coping with his identity crisis, an issue too difficult for him to face. Interestingly, none of the people he mentions having known are white. They are all young black men and women who see themselves as engaged in a struggle to assert their own identity, not unusual for people of color at academic institutions. In these one-dimensional depictions, the students appear as obsessed with race as he says he is. They are likely the composite characters that he references in the introduction, and they serve to highlight his personal need for belonging. One woman he meets is not interested in attending a Black Students' Association meeting because she is "not black," but "multiracial" of African, Native American, and Italian descent. She asks him a question that he may have wondered himself but never fully expressed, "Why should I have to choose?" He judges her harshly, lumping her into a composite "they": "they avoided black people" (*DFMF,* 99). His concluding thought about "people like Joyce" is that "they" assume a kind of privilege, one that allows "the half-breeds and the college-degreed" to assimilate into "white culture" and to leave behind the minority "losers" who cannot shed the negative image imposed on the entire group (*DFMF,* 100). This shift in pronoun usage is sure to place distance between his own attitude and Joyce's since he has already accepted black as a primary part of his identity. He expresses not only a fear of not belonging to the black race as well as his desire to identify as black because he desires to.

His relationship with the black students who have no choice but to be black is similar to that he had with Ray, but these students are more mature and politically aware. Marcus has what Obama describes as an "authentic black experience" (*DFMF*, 101). Authentic means that a black person has lived an experience steeped in struggle and, when possible, engaged politically to redefine his or her social position in America. Marcus's authentic lineage comes by way of his Garveyite grandfather and his single mother. Another student, Regina, comes from the South Side of Chicago, where she lived with a "struggling mother" in the absence of her father. His lack of experience with blacks moves him toward a tendency to romanticize and simplify blackness: "Her voice evoked a vision of black life in all its possibility, a vision that filled me with a longing—a longing for place, and a fixed and definite history" (*DFMF*, 104). His admission to Regina that he envies her memories makes her confess that she envies his upbringing in Hawaii. Interestingly, each person seems to avoid the fact that Barack possesses access to a personal history that most African Americans do not have—that is, the knowledge of the historical origins of his parents, especially his Luo father.

Regina, like no other "character" in this autobiography provides him with a place for him to go in America, a possible place to belong. The belonging begins in terms of his inner sense of self, akin to the self-creation that he speaks of in reference to Malcolm X. She helps him to find his voice: "I could feel it growing stronger, sturdier, that constant, honest portion of myself, a bridge between my future and my past" (*DFMF*, 105). He finds that he has become "hungry for words" (*DFMF*, 105). Obama has admitted to reading the works of African American male writers, and this revelation is almost an exact quote from Wright's *Black Boy*. According to the tradition, as we see it continuing here, this revelation regarding a "hunger" for words and its relation to voice marks a turning point in the life of the writer. All of the previous autobiographies I have discussed, winking to their readers in a sense, let us know the moment when they became what they were at the time their autobiographies were published and, in essence, what led to their being targeted by a press for the writing of their autobiographies. Similar to Frederick Douglass, Barack is given the chance to speak at a political rally that has been organized to bring attention to black people's confinement, in this case apartheid in South Africa. Before he goes on he recalls the power of speaking as he earlier observed it through his father's example when the elder Barack spoke to his classmates. However, we might also be reminded that his family has always depicted his father as capable of charming people with his verbal communication skills—the man in the bar, the attendees at the awards ceremony, his in-laws, his wife, and his angry son.

Barack's speech is successful, even though it was more than he was supposed to have given, but his fears about himself resurface. He grows angry about what he said, feeling that his words were self-centered and self-gratifying and not helpful to others. As a result of his feelings, he directs his fears and shame at Regina. At the heart of his argument with Regina is his deep-seated conflict regarding his biracial identity. For the most part he questions his right to speak on behalf of black folks. Regina tells him that his work for others is not about him but about the people whom he hopes to serve. One has to wonder here about a conversation that rings true about a man who, as a public figure, is constantly questioned about whether he is speaking on behalf of black folks.[9] While this conversation may be, to some degree, true—at best, we know that he is drinking beer and that Obama could not have been able to recall a conversation he had had with someone some twenty years earlier—it also seems more like a pontification of a subconscious conversation about his legitimacy. Obama may be probing his future at this point and asking important questions about the balance between how he uses his voice and how he should direct his career.

From there, Barack moves into his career as a community organizer in Chicago. The chapter preceding his move to Chicago only succeeds in setting the stage for telling his readers when and why he decided to go to Chicago after graduating from Columbia, which he attended after transferring from Occidental. We can easily surmise that his interactions with Regina and her memories of Chicago, a city he has identified as a place of belonging for black people, made the job offer in Chicago sound appealing. Yet, his experiences as an activist on campus, which forced

9. I reference early criticism during his presidential campaign by blacks, including the black media, about his representation of and understanding of black Americans.

him to think more of others and less of himself, would have also inspired him to look for such work, even when other black folks were telling him to concentrate further on excelling in his professional career. Ultimately, his need to belong to a race and to know what it meant to belong led him to work among black people.

One of the problems that Barack faces is indicative of the post–Civil Rights movement—that is the concern with balancing professional aspirations with community solidarity. Obama says that he had an early desire, one that none of his peers seemed to understand, to become involved in community work. This desire clashed with the opportunities that graduating from an Ivy League school would bring. His belief that he could effect change in the country by organizing black folks at the grass roots, a job that would yield very little income and much frustration, draws a response of "skepticism" from his peers (*DFMF,* 133). Even older black people look to him to gain power in the corporate world, which will make them proud and prove the success of the movement that was to allow all people opportunities to be successful. Why, they ask, would someone who has the chance to do better than people of the previous generation not take advantage of it? In retrospect, he explains that his reasoning started with his "father and his father before him" and other parts of his personal narrative described in *Dreams*—"his mother and parents, beggars in Indonesia, his college friends, his father's death" (*DFMF,* 134). Though he did not grow up in the abject poverty that the earlier black autobiographers describe as their "black" experience, he reasons that he is aware of the experience. It would seem then that he hoped to locate himself in history by asserting himself in a memorable effective way. Ultimately, I would argue that since Obama begins and ends by acknowledging his father, at this juncture, he is striving to make choices about the type of black man that he wants to be. Since he cannot, nor has he shown a desire to, define himself as other than a black man, he will have to determine what it means to be black in the United States, particularly in the era when the idea of blackness has broadened. By engaging in these activities, he may also learn more about the experiences and motivations of the black man whom he was only to know for a month at the age of ten.

As a man who came to age in the decade just after the Civil Rights movement began, Obama poses questions about where black folks are and where they hope to go. Throughout *Dreams,* Obama makes many references to the Civil Rights movement. When he refers to his days as a college activist he recalls images of college students before him, specifically North Carolina Agricultural and Technological students at the Greensboro Woolworth's and SNCC voting rights activists, noting that "such images became a form of prayer for me, bolstering my spirits" (*DFMF,* 134). Earlier, in the introduction of the 2004 edition of the book, he places his victory as the third African American since Reconstruction to have been elected to the United States Senate as part of a Civil Rights victory, noting the bitter truth of its occurrence fifty years after *Brown* and forty years after the Voting Rights Act (*DFMF,* ix). Though his primary concern is with his own personal struggle to define his identity in America, or to satisfy his "need for a race," there are lingering questions about the role that black people of his generation should possess. If this is a journey to knowing about the self, the self is connected to a larger community, Obama strongly suggests, that may or may not have the answers that the individual seeks. We see his seeking answers about the role of the post–Civil Rights black when he attends a talk by the "black power" activist Kwame Ture. According to Obama, Ture was advocating for an economic relationship between Africa and Harlem (*DFMF,* 140). Finding Ture's Black Nationalism advocacy to be problematic and largely unsatisfactory, Obama concludes, "The movement had died years ago, shattered into a thousand fragments" (*DFMF,* 140). What then should be the new direction as he prepares to move to Chicago to assume a position as an organizer of blacks?

The South Side of Chicago is where he finds the answer to the question. Though he has not spent much time in black communities, he knows that this is his opportunity to learn about black Americans. There is no better place for his lessons to begin than in a black-owned barbershop. In the shop, among black men of the South Side, he learns of blacks' feelings about the newly elected black mayor whom everyone refers to fondly, and simply, as Harold. His desire for a place of belonging is common in works written by black men as these places offer security to some and authentication for others. We may consider Hughes's journey to Harlem, where he could be among black folks despite his father's protests. Malcolm X also moves to Harlem, but not before he engages black men in a pool hall several years earlier in Roxbury. Wright leaves Jackson and heads straight for Beale Street in Tennessee and later to northern black communities. These black men, of course, had very little choice about where they could go because of segregation, but none of them show any reluctance about finding refuge in the economically challenged areas of black communities. The barbershop patrons' feelings about the black mayor are acknowledged by Obama's "writer self": "Within the black community, there was a sense of pride regarding my accomplishment, a pride mingled with frustration" (*DFMF*, viii–ix). Chicago's black mayor brings a sense of empowerment to the black residents of Chicago, and Obama, the future congressman and presidential hopeful, is able to witness a black pride movement, so to speak, that he did not witness growing up—the advent of a black man who brings hope to a people in need.

His entrance into this era leaves him wide open to what Chicago's South Side can gain from his leadership and and what the black community can offer him by way of experience. One of the first lessons he learns is that in order to penetrate the community, he must align himself with the black churches. Often, Obama appears cynical about the black men he meets. Reverend Smalls is one of those people. Accordingly, he is presented as a black preacher who is not willing to join forces with any rival leaders, and in fact, he seems to highlight the overwhelming concern that all of the black pastors may have about who appears to be in charge. If they are following, and not leading, they may lose their members to the leaders. Significantly, Barack finds himself moving within the conflicted relationships that were present during the Civil Rights movement as well. Among the concerns were who would lead the people and how they would be led. Reverend Smalls discourages the other pastors from joining the organization that Barack works for but later calls him to participate in the grand-opening event that the mayor has agreed to attend. Obama's description reveals a weakness in black communities among clergy, whom black people would rather see as the people helping them to, at the least, cope with the problems of economic deprivation and social injustice.

His observations eventually blend with active communal engagements. Barack, following the advice of his white boss, Marty, learns about the people themselves. Despite the fact that Marty also tells him later to "build a life for [himself] outside the job" he becomes part of the community, noting that he went to the bars with the men after the meetings, attended Sunday services, danced with the women at Christmas parties, mentored sons and daughters, bounced their grandchildren on his knee

(*DFMF,* 187–88). Within a year, he recalls a comment made by a woman named Shirley, which makes him feel like "a sort of surrogate prodigal son" (*DFMF,* 227). However, he still feels haunted by what inspired him to become an organizer of black people in a black community: "Wandering through Altgeld or other tough neighborhoods, my fears were also internal: the old fears of not belonging" (*DFMF,* 253). He goes on to make clear that he was not concerned with physical assault, as others who did belong may have been, but of not being accepted by the black race represented by the South Side community.

As I noted earlier, Barack's search for a black identity among these people is not solely an individual search; he sees his own experience as aligned with that of black folks from the past as well as with that of people younger than he. It is no wonder then that he tries to act as a mentor to Kyle, a maturing black teenager who is also without a father. The role Barack attempts to play is that of guide and confidant who is struggling to find his own way. Since we see Kyle through Obama's eyes, it would seem that Kyle is not struggling for racial acceptance as is his mentor. Instead, Kyle is struggling to define himself as a man. His struggle becomes pronounced on the basketball court when an opponent calls him a "punk." Kyle's response of punching the man and rebuffing his label with a voice that "trembled," reveals his need to be seen not as a "punk" but as a masculine being (*DFMF,* 255). Kyle's problem may be in the hearts of many of the young black men whom Barack notices. He begins to observe a generation of black men, some of whom react violently to one another and leave other residents fearing for their lives. He records two instances: in one, young black men run past residents while shooting at another young man; a second occurs when Barack walks outside one late night and asks some young men in a car to turn down their music as they are disturbing him and others. At this moment he realizes that he and the generation he physically turns his back to are not the same. Again, the idea of the Civil Rights movement is diminished and a new plan needs to be constructed if the next generation is to indulge the hopes of the past. Only by engaging in the life of the community is he able to have any kind of a realization about where its people—his people—stand.

Part of what he sees as the problem is what he knows best—the absent black father. He finds this when he focuses on the school system, which by this time is not suffering from segregation but is instead run by blacks and largely attended by black children. Among the problems detrimental to the system's success are a high dropout rate, lack of attention by the community's educators, who send their children to private schools, and major annual budget problems. Among those trying to make sure that the children are not victims of the system is Asante Moran. Asante proves to be the first black American man in *Dreams* who has a connection to Africa that intrigues Barack, a man whose own personal connection to Africa has been largely unexplored. Asante believes that a real education for black children should give him an understanding "of *himself, his* world, *his* culture, *his* community" (*DFMF,* 258). His ideas are likely the results of the 1960s Black Power movement during which Afrocentrism began to form in black communities. Interestingly, much of what he is saying—for as much as we can believe the author's recollection of the conversation—speaks almost directly to what was absent in the writer's life. He proceeds to tell him that the girls are not as vulnerable as the boys because of the presence of older black women.[10] The concern is with the boys, half of whom, he notes, do not know their own fathers. He goes on to say,

> There's nobody to guide them through the process of becoming a man
> . . . to explain to them the meaning of manhood. And that's a recipe
> for disaster. Because in every society, young men are going to have vi-
> olent tendencies. Either those tendencies are directed and disciplined
> in creative pursuits or those tendencies destroy the young men, or the
> society, or both. (*DFMF,* 258)

I quote this passage at length because it seems to point more to a personal revelation about the self, the "I" as opposed to one of the community even though his experience overlaps with theirs. Asante's own sense of himself illuminates the need Barack has to learn about himself, his culture, and his community, and more significantly, the meaning of manhood. This conversation ends with Asante telling him that he should go to Africa because it would change Barack's life as it had his. The meeting's end causes Barack to reflect back on the father who abandoned

10. Though the focus of their "conversation" and this autobiography is clearly on father-son relationships, the importance of the father-daughter relationship should not be dismissed or devalued.

him, first in life and then in death, leaving him to communicate with his father through the memories of others and in his dreams.

Dreams from My Father, as the title suggests, speaks to the determined efforts of a man trying to connect with his father on a level that is not directly physical. There is a relationship that exists largely in the mind of the son and is constructed based on what he has learned from his mother and grandparents, his sister, Auma, and his paternal family, his childhood memories of a month's visit and subsequent correspondence during this adolescence; these, perhaps, result in dreams that he has about his father or from his father. The dream, as he describes it, comes a year after he learns about his father's death. He relays that he feels "no pain, only the vague loss of an opportunity" (*DFMF,* 128). Obama's sentiment is reminiscent of Frederick Douglass's reference to how he felt about hearing the news of his mother's death; his too is an expressionless idea of pain. One has to wonder how a son that had grieved the absence of his father for so many years and had searched for him by forming relationships with blacks in the hope of having an experience of acceptance could feel no pain whatsoever over the death of his father. Based on the ending of *Dreams* where he cries at his father's grave, it would seem that he was unable to articulate the pain of his loss, for death means more than a loss of an opportunity for him, it also means that he will never know, on a personal level, his father and how it feels to be accepted by him. The dream that he describes as having a year after his father's death reveals the lingering need, a haunting of sorts, to have a connection with his father. He dreams of taking a journey that ends with his releasing his father from a jail cell. Though he has not yet journeyed to Kenya to visit his father's grave and learn more about his family history, he has been engaged in a quest—a proverbial trip or journey—that has been largely focused on his identity as a black man, and his father's absence has exacerbated his need to engage in the search. He finds his father, then, in a place where he has been confined emotionally and in an emotional state. Barack has matured enough, a year after his father's death, that he can confront his feelings and cry in his father's presence and perhaps forgive him for his emotional, if not his physical, absence in his life. Therefore, after he releases him from the jail cell, they embrace, and as Barack cries, his father tells him that he loves him. Interestingly, in this dream the son feels that his father is "small . . . the size of a boy" (*DFMF,* 129). Ultimately, the son accepts the father from whom he has distanced himself emotionally. And, as in the cases of Hughes, Wright, and Malcolm X, his critique of his father's weaknesses allows him to emerge as an adult who rises above his father as an emotionally mature man and thus, the stronger of the two.

This dream suggests a search for understanding, a desire to achieve wholeness, and, ultimately, the need to feel loved. Further, *Dreams* reveals a search for a spiritual connection that transcends the individual and connects to the larger majority, including the black race and, at times, the human race. Barack's focus in this direction is revealed by his feelings when he listens to the sermon "Audacity of Hope." Barack does not make clear how he feels about religion. When asked about his congregational affiliation he answers that he visits churches. For the most part, Obama speaks rather cynically about the black male preachers, casting them as men who seem more concerned with themselves and advancing their self-centered reputations than with meeting the needs of their congregations. On this particular Sunday, after a child asks "Where is God?" he has a moment of revelation during Reverend Wright's sermon.[11] Obama evokes the religious tradition depicted in African American writing through his description of the singing, shouting, and preaching, such as in the works of Richard Wright and James Baldwin. This author observes that the sermon is "a mediation on a fallen world," in reference to people of various classes with black people becoming the primary subject for these experiences. He imagines black folks in churches across the city and wonders how their stories merged with those of biblical characters such as, for example, David and Goliath. Like them, black people could indulge in the spirit of hope together: "Those stories—of survival, and freedom, and hope—became our story, my story; the blood that had spilled was our blood" (*DFMF*, 294). For the first time in *Dreams*, through Barack's experiences Obama expresses a feeling that he has achieved wholeness—that is a connection and sense of belonging to the race that he felt disconnected from for most of his life. Before he expressed feeling a connection with people of the community, but at this point he feels that the connection has grown to include the race. For him, it is, significantly, a spiritual connection: "I also felt for the first time how the spirit

11. By the time he published *Dreams* he was a member of the church; however, during his presidential campaign, Obama publicly broke from the church, citing comments from Reverend Wright about America.

carried within it, nascent, incomplete, the possibility of moving beyond our narrow dreams" (*DFMF,* 294). His realization that he has this connection with other black folks means that he is ready to move on to the next level—connecting with his lost father by visiting Kenya.

In the next chapter, I will explore the relevance of his visit to Kenya and its connection to healing the wounds of paternal abandonment. It is clear at this point, however, that Obama was a man consumed with defining himself as a black man in America. He has also become a man who has made conscious efforts to avoid following his father's path. He states, "Someone once said that every man is trying to either live up to his father's expectations or make up for his father's mistakes, and I suppose that may explain my particular malady as anything else."[12] Autobiography is a healing tool for the author, but, if allowed, it can also be a tool for exploring and publicly evaluating issues. Obama makes clear, in this continuation of black male autobiographical writing, that black fathers are essential. The absence of Obama Sr. from his son's life forced his son to look to other men, and women, to affirm his racial identity. As he tells his story, he seems to find his footing only through his interactions with the race that accepts him, despite his greatest fears of rejection. Obama, then, shows the possibilities of escaping the pressures of social pitfalls as much as he proves the importance of black communities in the late twentieth century providing homes for those wandering black sons in need of understanding, healing, and love.

12. Obama, *Audacity of Hope,* 3.

Chapter Five

The Sons Return to Africa

What is Africa to me?

. . . .

Strong bronzed men or regal black
Women from whose loins I sprang

. . . .

—Countee Cullen, "Heritage"

W. E. B. Du Bois identifies the conflict of the "unreconciled strivings" among African Americans to balance the struggle of being both a person of African descent and an American. As a result of this struggle, African Americans experience feelings of homelessness. The struggle appears pronounced in the works of Langston Hughes, Richard Wright, Malcolm X, and Barack Obama. Not only do the men attempt to define themselves as black men in America, but that struggle involves a feeling of being rejected by America, which has often responded to its black citizens with traumatic violence. Thus, it is no surprise that the personal narratives of the black men I examine here speak of a fear of violence: Hughes fears what may happen to him in the South; Wright is threatened by coworkers in Memphis; Malcolm X anticipates dying a violent death, as did his father and uncles; Obama references his father's relationship with his mother as life-threatening and barely legal. Their upbringing in a culture of violence made them long for a place where racially motivated attacks would not impede their freedom.

Africa represents that hope. With the exception of Obama, whose father was East African, the men had no direct familial connections with Africa. They did not return to a literal home, as Obama did, with relatives there to greet them at the airport or recognize their names as having specific histories. These three men's surnames had been changed to reflect the history of slavery in the United States; thus, the specifics of their personal histories are unknown to the men. Since much is unknown, the three black American men possess a desire to try to cobble together an understanding about cultures unknown to them by visiting West Africa. The men go to Africa seeking reconciliation of the self, which entails African Americans' hope that they will be accepted by Africans and be able to reclaim a home and sense of a racial self. Acceptance involves recognition not only on the part of Africans that the African American seeking acceptance is of African descent, but also that he has retained a connection to Africa that goes beyond mere skin color. It is here that the search for self and home becomes prominent. If the African American is exiled in the United States, an exploration of the African self would mean establishing an understanding of the racialized self as an American.

At the heart of community is acceptance. Often when we think of black communities we think of geographical areas where people live, sometimes for generations. The neighborhoods themselves may have histories within the cities or towns that instill fond memories in some and are marks of shame to others. We may consider not only the descriptions of the black men's engagements in these communities, but also those presented in the literature of Zora Neale Hurston, Toni Morrison, Gloria Naylor, and Ann Petry. Black communities as geographical places may also be fluid, as people located there may leave and relocate elsewhere, either in other black communities or in integrated communities. When entering a community, both children and adults may feel a sense of dread that the community will not be welcoming as we see in Wright's *Black Boy,* when young Richard fights the children to get to the grocery store, or in Obama's *Dreams,* when Barack moves to Chicago's South Side. Trying to locate the black self, then, within America is not just the determination of how to deal with racism; it also involves how to communicate with other blacks, in essence, how "to fit in." The personal narratives of the four men I have discussed reveal how this struggle occurs in American black communities and in Africa as well.

My concern in this chapter is with exploring why the four men visited Africa. Each man had specific reasons for his visit. What they learned as a result of their visits varies. However, as African American men who were engaged in tenuous relationships with America, their visits to Africa were intensely personal. Each man sought to learn more about what might or might not be absent: his cultural connection to a continent on which he was not born but with which he had always been associated, whether he wanted to be or not. Because their fathers abandoned them either through desertion or death, these men's need for belonging and acceptance, I argue, is more pronounced. Their longing to fill a void left by their fathers' absence inspires them to visit Africa and to make a determination about their place beyond America by, returning to the land of their fathers.

African Americans began to develop ties with Africa during the Civil Rights movement and the parallel West African independence movements. According to Kevin Gaines, Ghana's successful movement for independence from British rule was a significant triumph among people of African descent across the globe: "Ghana's independence lent momentum to rising demands for freedom and self-determination and heralded the impending demise of the systems of racial and colonial domination instituted in the late nineteenth century in the US South and on the African continent."[1] Present at the celebratory ceremonies were dignitaries from the Caribbean, America, Europe, and the United States, including Vice President Richard Nixon, George Padmore, C. L. R. James, Adam Clayton Powell, and Martin Luther King Jr.[2] Ghana would become a haven for black American expatriates looking for a black nation that would respect their right to freedom.

Langston Hughes, an African American world traveler and internationally known writer, had always considered Africa in his poetry. Du Bois's observation that the Negro struggle to merge an African self with an American self was a prominent concern in the literature of Harlem Renaissance writers, as Cullen's persona expresses in his poem. "What

1. Kevin Kelley Gaines, *Americans in Ghana: Black Expatriates and the Civil Rights Movement*, 2.
2. Ibid., 5.

is Africa to me?" is a question that Hughes had asked and answered many times in his own poetry and life. In Hughes's autobiography, *The Big Sea,* the struggle for an African American identity was personal. Born the only son to parents of mixed ancestry—African, European, and Native American—Hughes's identity as an African American male, as I have discussed, was challenged by his father's alarming feelings about "niggers," which included any person of African descent in America. While Cullen's "Heritage" persona rejects an African identity, Hughes's poetry and activism advances his desire to move beyond his existence as an American man of African descent and embrace a global identity rooted in Africa.

Hughes's embrace of his racial identity was furthered by his interactions with black communities all over the country and in different parts of the world. His visit to the South allows him to confront his fears that a black man is almost sure to die a violent death there. In order to truly fit into the South he must embrace rather than deny his African heritage. He does this in Louisiana by engaging in conversation with blacks in Baton Rouge and visiting blues clubs in New Orleans. He also visits black universities as part of a tour organized by Mary McLeod Bethune.

Hughes makes conscious efforts to learn more about the identity of the persona he creates in "Negro Speaks of Rivers." When Hughes first visits Africa as a member of a ship's crew, his description of the continent is straightforward. According to Hughes they visit thirty-two ports along the West Coast.[3] He observes "white men with guns at their belts, inns and taverns with signs up, EUROPEANS ONLY, missionary churches with the Negroes in the back seats."[4] He also observes a young African female prostitute raped by his crewmates.[5] Hughes is critical of his crewmates and the colonial system and sympathetic to black Africans suffering under oppression. In Senegal he tries to connect with one man by noting that our problems are "very much like yours, especially in the South. I am a Negro too," he declares. His attempt to see their experience as West Africans through an American lens, even a racialized lens, is met with laughter, he says, because of his light skin.[6] To them, he is American and not African.

3. Ibid., 106.
4. Ibid.
5. Ibid., 108.
6. Ibid., 102.

Though he does not state it, he most certainly implies that he had hoped to establish an identity as a son of Africa. As early as 1921, when he published "The Negro Speaks of Rivers," Hughes affirms the desire to balance the two consciousnesses as African and America. Most certainly the "I" in this poem connects him to the cultural history that his father rejects. Not only does his poetic voice personalize the experiences of bathing, building, and hearing, thereby claiming them as his own, but through the poem he also links the "I" to Africa and to the American South—a link that will prove important for négritude writers. Hughes's decision to embrace and celebrate the very history that his father despises is a significant step toward gaining emotional independence, asserting manhood, and affirming a racial identity. During the 1920s, Hughes's poetic sense of Africa dealt more with the integration of African cultures into African American culture. For Hughes, Africa's presence in the United States was more of a celebration as evidenced in his poem" "Danse Africane," where he concentrates on artistic expression. The poem focuses on a girl dancing to the "tom-tom" beats.

As a result of his earlier poem, Hughes eventually receives recognition and acceptance as a black by Africans. Edward Ako notes Hughes's influence as a Harlem Renaissance poet on the négritude writers "who had been told that it was a matter of great speculation as to whether the monkey descended from the African or the African from the monkey, . . . [and] suddenly realized that over in the United States a group of writers were singing the beauty of black women, affirming their humanity, looking nostalgically at the warm tropical Africa from which they had been stolen."[7] In response to Hughes and other Harlem Renaissance writers, the négritude African and Caribbean writers applied Hughes's black beauty aesthetic to the creation of their own literature. When Leopold Senghor, a Senegalese négritude poet, spoke at Howard University in 1966, he credited Hughes with inspiring négritude: "Before being an ideology, an idea, negritude is first of all a fact. It was Langston Hughes who wrote, shortly after World War 1: 'We younger Negro artists who create now intend to express our individual dark-skinned selves without fear or shame.'"[8] Hughes's essay "The Negro Artist and the

7. Edward Ako, "Langston Hughes and the Négritude Movement: A Study in Literary Influences," 49.
8. Ibid., 55.

Racial Mountain" was a call not only to young black artists in America, but also clearly to would-be black artists abroad. Lilyan Kestleoot argues that these writers essentially prove that Hughes's poetry was the foundation of the négritude movement. She states, "American literature already contained seeds of the main themes of negritude. Hence, one can assert that the real *fathers* of the Negro cultural renaissance in France were neither traditional West Indian writers, nor the French surrealist poets, nor the French novelists of the two wars, but black writers of the United States."[9] Through these later poets, Hughes's celebration of an African American identity became the inspiration for other African identities. As a young poet, he had unwittingly laid the foundation for a global black aesthetic movement.

Though these writers felt connected to Hughes, he had become disconnected from Africa. In 1954, Hughes became reacquainted with Africa when the assistant editor of *Drum*, Africa's leading magazine, asked him to judge its international short story competition. Previous to this reintroduction to the land of his racial subconscious, Hughes admitted that he "had no contact with Africa, no reliable, fresh knowledge of the land he had visited in 1923."[10] According to Arnold Rampersad, his contacts between 1923 and 1954 did, however, include poets involved with the literary magazine *Presence Africaine*. Rampersad reveals further that at least three African writers wrote about how much they admired Hughes's celebration of blackness.[11] Hughes would later define négritude in terms of how he understood his own poetry: "To us négritude was an unknown word, but certainly pride of heritage and consciousness of race was ingrained in us."[12] We should certainly note here that his renewed relationship with Africa in response to attention to his work corresponds with the independence movements in West Africa.

While Hughes may not have been immediately aware of his impact on the négritude writers, once he affirms his part in inspiring the movement, he becomes directly involved in promoting literature by Africans and about Africa. In 1960, Hughes found a publisher for *An African Treasurer: Articles, Essays, Stories, Poems by Black Africans*, an anthology of fiction

9. Lilyan Kestleoot, "Negritude and Its American Sources," 5, emphasis mine.
10. Rampersad, *Life*.
11. Ibid.
12. Langston Hughes, "The Twenties: Harlem and Its Negritude," 472.

and nonfiction written by African writers whom he hoped would become known in the United States. In his poem "We, Too," he asserts the idea of a diasporic brotherhood that is rooted in oppression. He writes, "Oh, Congo brother / We, too emit a frightening cry / From body scarred / Soul that won't die."[13] This poem takes us back to the ideas of his 1925 poem "I, Too" where he asserts his presence in America as the "darker brother" and his earliest poem, "The Negro Speaks of Rivers," where he emits a sense of racial consciousness bound by the soul—the "essence of the Negro."[14] Hughes asserts that the experience of one member of the African diaspora, regardless of the space he or she occupies, is that of all. In fact, he published a series of poems after 1951 that grew increasingly political in their reaction to South African apartheid and colonialism, and they are marked by his perspective as an African American. Poems such as "In Explanation of Our Times," which celebrates "The folks with no titles in front of their names / all over the world" who were asserting their independence from colonial rule.[15] This poem not only marked the independence movements in Africa and Asia, but also historicized these movements led by oppressed peoples. In this sense, the poem did not give voice so much as it celebrated emerging voices.

Hughes embraced his reception by négritude writers and proudly acknowledged the impact that he and other writers of his day had on them: "In France as well as Germany, before the close of the Negro Renaissance, Harlem's poets were already being translated" by Léopold Sedar Senghor of Senegal and Aime Césaire of Martinique.[16] In several essays written between 1960 and 1967, Hughes places himself and his poetry in the midst of the négritude movement. The impact of the poet's early career is acknowledged when he travels to Dakar, Senegal, in March 1966 as a leader of an American delegation appointed by President Lyndon B. Johnson. There he is honored by President Senghor for his influences on him and others.[17] In his 1966 speech "Black Writers in a Troubled World," Hughes says that "The Negro Speaks of Rivers" was an example of the themes of both the Harlem Renaissance and the

---

13. Arnold Rampersad, ed., *The Collected Poems of Langston Hughes*, 538.
14. Ibid., 533.
15. Ibid., 449.
16. Hughes, "The Twenties," 471.
17. Rampersad, ed., *Collected Poems*, 19.

négritude. He observes, "Negritude has its roots deep in the beauty of black people—in what the younger writers and musicians in America call 'soul' which I would define in this way: Soul is the synthesis of the essence of Negro folk art redistilled—particularly the old music and its flavor, the ancient basic beat out of Africa, the folk rhymes and Ashanti stories."[18] He goes on to say, "Soul is contemporary Harlem's negritude, revealing to the Negro people and the world the beauty within themselves. I once tried to say that in a poem, 'The Negro Speaks of Rivers.'"[19] An emerging theme of the poem is the enduring nature of the soul that maintains a continuum from Africa to America. The soul then, is the essence of the culture that he sees as present among black folks, regardless of the location of the black body.

It may be argued that Hughes develops a paternal relationship with the younger male generation of West Africans. In the 1960s, the fatherless child, according to Rampersad, sought paternal relationships with some of his younger African protégés. He began a relationship with a young African man. This relationship does not flourish, but apparently the one he developed with a young policeman he met in Lagos did, as Hughes named the young African man as a major beneficiary in his will.[20] Rampersad does not see Hughes as a literary father, stating, "Surfacing now perhaps, at last, was the observe self-image, which had been latent in him from the start—his sense of himself, in his most intimate role as poet, as mother (hardly a father) to the race, rather than its princely child."[21] He suggests here that Hughes, like a mother, birthed and nurtured a movement. Certainly Hughes did see himself as at least partially responsible for uncovering the culture that had been lying beneath centuries of abuse—which resulted for too many years in the denial of blackness as connected to beauty. However, I believe his "self-image" is largely the result of his father's belief that black was synonymous with oppression. To be black, an identity his father denied, and to be American in a country his father loathed demonstrates Hughes's greatest desire to be that independent, black proud father he wants others of his race to be.

18. Langston Hughes, "Black Writers in a Troubled World," 477.
19. Langston Hughes, "The Negro Speaks of Rivers," 477.
20. Arnold Rampersad, *Life*, 240.
21. Ibid.

Hughes may embrace a connection with Africa, but Wright teeters between claiming a connection and denying it. Critics have attempted to assess Wright's intent regarding the purpose, whether successfully asserted or not, of *Black Power*. Ngwarsungu Chiwengo argues, "While African American identity is the overriding theme of this travel book, Wright, the socially-defined man of color, perceptively understands that his own image and that of the African are co-dependent."[22] Kevin Gaines states, "Modernity rather than diaspora formed the key concept in *Black Power* and Wright's other writings from that period."[23] I argue that Wright works from the influences of modernity as well as that of a conflicted African American trying to define his identity as a man of African descent in a Western world.

Wright titles his observations of the Gold Coast during Kwame Nkrumah's movement for an independent African country in 1953 *Black Power*. Ironically, this phrase will be made popular by Stokely Carmichael in the 1960s. Carmichael, who would later move to Africa and become known as Kwame Ture, used the phrase to refer to a black nationalist agenda that would preference the presence and work of blacks over whites in black communities. It was his belief that blacks could empower themselves in this way. Carmichael's use of the term aptly describes both the black American focus and Nkrumah's movement.

The title, however, originally centered on an Africa Wright did not know and not on an America that he had known too well. As a result of his clash of knowledge, so to speak, when Wright visited Africa, he felt his "twoness":

The American Negro's passionate identification with America stemmed from two considerations: first, it was a natural part of his assimilation of Americanism; second, so long had Africa been described as something shameful, barbaric, a land in which one went about naked, a land in which his ancestors sold his kith and kin as slaves— so long had he heard all this that he wanted to disassociate himself in his mind from all such realities.[24]

---

22. Ngwarsungu Chiwengo, "Richard Wright's Africa," 44.

23. Gaines, *Americans in Ghana*, 54.

24. Richard Wright, *Black Power*, 72, hereinafter cited parenthetically in the text with the abbreviation *BP.*

Wright not only describes myths about Africa, which made blacks want to separate themselves from Africa and embrace America, but he goes on to express his personal dilemma with the myths:

> "The bafflement evoked in me by this new reality did not spring from any desire to disclaim kinship with Africa, or from any shame of being of African descent. My problem was how to account for this 'survival' of Africa in America" (*BP,* 73).

Interestingly, Wright, who was at this time a resident, though not a citizen of Paris, inquires as to how the African part of him can live in unity with that part of him that is American *in America.*

Before looking at what Wright says of how he feels about Africa, I would like to probe the question of why he decided to visit Africa, particularly the Gold Coast. According to Wright in the first chapter of the travelogue, after a dinner at his home, Dorothy, wife of George Padmore the West Indian Pan-Africanist, asks Wright, "Why don't you go to Africa?" (*BP,* 3). It is interesting that before coming to the suggestive question that eventually leads to his trip to the Gold Coast, Wright introduces the scene as having occurred on Easter Sunday in his home that over-looks "the gray walls of the University of Paris" which he can see as he looks out of a window (*BP,* 3). The backdrop for this conversation appears as a fitting introduction to the perspective that he offers in *Black Power* that is laced with his lifestyle as a writer-in-residence in Paris, his new home after having exiled himself from the United States in 1947 and having abandoned the Communist Party. All of these—his American point of view, his Paris experiences, his interest in Communism and Marxism, and his love/hate relationship with religion—are present in his interpretations of the successes of African way of life as well as what he will consider failures.

Wright goes on to consider the reasons for visiting Africa. Padmore tells him that Kwame Nkrumah is leading the movement for independence, but Wright says that their talk was overshadowed by his "mind and feelings" (*BP,* 4). As does Hughes, he wonders about his relationship to Africa; in doing so, he admits that he is "of African descent" but is not sure "whether or not he would be able to feel and know something about Africa on the basis of a common 'racial' heritage" (*BP,* 4). He goes on to admit to other parts of his racial make-up that include European eth-

nicities. The question of identity lingers: *"But, am I African?" (BP,* 4). Determining the answer to this question will prove to be a major focus of
Black Power and is likely the very reason Wright decides that he will indeed visit the Gold Coast. His decision to visit then is intensely personal
and seems to have little to do with the issues raised by Dorothy Padmore
and Wright's wife regarding the changing political status of Gold Coast,
today known as Ghana. Notably, he does not consider the fact that he
will be visiting a country at the time of the country's proposed transition
of power—a historical, momentous event. Instead he thinks of the Gold
Coast as representative of the continent of Africa, a place not of nations
but one where cultural roots lie.

Wright's feelings prove conflicted as he fluctuates between his personal
perspective of the people whom he observes and the political movement
that he critiques. Surely, Wright has always combined the political with
the intensely personal in his observations of black life, but here, Wright's
dilemma regarding whether he is at all African dominates his work.
Wright opens by giving information about his political position, "In pre-
senting this picture of a part of Africa, I openly use, to a limited degree,
Marxist analysis of historic events to explain what has happened in this
world . . . (*BP,* xxxvii–xxxviii). At this point he also informs readers that
he was a member of the Communist Party of the United States from
1932 to 1944 and explains how that experience influences his current
convictions which he renders in *Black Power.* Rather than rely on his own
perspective to critique what he sees, he uses Marxist theorists to discuss
Africa and its history. Wright uses political and historical languages to
avoid articulating feelings that he would rather not confront and discuss
in *Black Power.*

Though Wright speaks from a political perspective here, it is impossible to overlook the emotions that he says arise when he is first approached with the idea of visiting Africa. Further, even though Wright
refers to himself as an "uneasy member" of the "Western world" as early
as the introduction, he seems oblivious to how much he is part of this
world. He notes, "The Western world does not even yet quite know how
hard and inhuman its face looks to those who live outside of its confines"
(*BP,* xxxvi–xxxvii). At one point Wright does question whether his assessment of "the African," as he frequently refers to the people of the
Gold Coast, is tainted by his views as an outsider, but he does not pursue this inquiry.

Wright focuses much of his time on attempting to learn about the people of the Gold Coast, and in doing so, he makes the inevitable attempt to learn more about himself as a person of African descent. When contemplating a visit, he asks, "[H]ad three hundred years imposed a psychological distance between me and the 'racial stock' from which I had sprung?" (*BP,* 4). Once there, he seems intent on learning the answer to that question based on his observations of African mannerisms. One such observation strikes him as fascinating when he sees women dancing and recalls that he had seen similar dancing in American "in storefront churches . . . in unpainted wooden prayer-meeting houses on the plantations of the Deep South" (*BP,* 62). It would appear that Wright's understanding of African cultural practices can only be advanced through a comparison of his "home" experiences—those that involve his rearing in the black South. As I have stated earlier and will reiterate here, Wright left the community of the South but could never emotionally or psychologically separate himself from it. However, Wright wonders about his connection to dancing, concluding, "Never in my life had I been unable to dance even a few elementary steps" (*BP,* 62). He goes on to admit that he had wanted to engage in the cultural practices when in the United States since they had been part of his environment, but "*had never been able to!*" (*BP,* 63). Wright admits here that he had not rejected such actions, but he felt the actions had rejected him. In essence, he believes that he did not possess the ability, despite his desire.

Other "African survivals" such as laughter "that bent the knee and turned the head," "shuffling of the feet" to express satisfaction or agreement, and an "inexplicable, almost sullen silence" in expression of disagreement or opposition catches Wright's attention, yet he continuously questions the idea of their survival among a race of people. Perhaps he questions the significance of these similarities because he has not engaged in all of the cultural practices that are believed to be part of Africa and of African descendants' lives, or perhaps he does not find a satisfactory answer to the question. Whatever the case, Wright's indecision about what he seeks in his conscious observations and comparisons, on the one hand, and what he denies, on the other hand, proves his dilemma regarding his double-consciousnesses as well as his privileged identity as a writer who resides in Paris. At this point, Wright has established in much of his work his fear of becoming victim to the institutions that led to his father's failures, as Wright perceived them, and probably his mother's failed health as well as other social problems that he felt were African Americans' by nature of birth. His movement from the South and America leaves him feeling the need to account for his own position and to define his identity. To a degree he briefly admits to the problem of a racial definition:

> "My problem was how to account for this 'survival' of Africa in America when I stoutly denied the mystic influence of 'race,' when I was certain as I was of being alive that it was only, by large, in the concrete social frame of reference in which men lived that one could account for men being what they were" (*BP,* 115).

He would rather attribute any similarities among a people to social locations. Cultures exist, yes, but race is questionable. How have African ways of life transferred and transformed to America among the people of African descent? And, as with Wright's lack of rhythm, how can they simply disappear? Notably, Wright, through practice in writing, has established some forms of expression that he feels are distinctly black in his writing, including Negro dialect and Christian practices found in churches and as influences in everyday life.

Black Power is yet another example of his attentiveness to what he deems cultural, if not racial, attributes—in particular the integration of religion as a form of cultural expression. Wright relates the women's dancing to American religious expressions and not to a more likely comparison such as that of secular dancing. His interest in religion, which continued as he was immersed in religious practices and beliefs from the time he wondered about his father's hope for a "call" to his conflicts with his religious grandmother over embracing it, remains a prominent concern in this narrative as well. Wright says that one reason for visiting the Gold Coast is to see the non-Christian people. Wright makes his observations of religion both Christian and "heathen" based on his own rejection of Christianity, which stems from his childhood. On his voyage to Ghana, he tells a Nigerian judge "I'm nothing in matters religious" (*BP,* 23). Yet, he frequently engages in religious observations. He may reject the beliefs, but in some ways he indulges the practice.

His indulgence of religious ceremonies, including Christian events, informs his curiosity. In the beginning of the narrative when Wright contemplates his visit he says that he wants to "see the pagans" because he knows "what a Christian African would have to say." Wright regards himself as "areligous," but he is drawn to the expression of religion practice. This is why Wright cannot keep himself from a Christian church. He confesses, "I preferred the religion I looked at to be interesting, with some of the real mystery, dread, and agony of existence" (*BP,* 148). Absent from the visit is the interesting part, for Wright, "the sexual suggestiveness" in the singing "which American Negroes manage to inject into their praises to God" (*BP,* 147). In fact, Wright laments the absence of what he deems an African Americanism, inspiring him to recall Paul Laurence Dunbar's "When Malindy Sings," a poem celebrating the beauty of a black woman's voice and the feelings evoked by her singing. His reference to Dunbar is a rare instance in which he makes an overt reference to a black writer as opposed to making literary illusions to European philosophers and American white writers as he had in his earlier works. The lack of comparison between cultures forces him to focus on the difference and makes him feel more like a black American than simply a man of the West.

In addition to recording the clash of his religious background with his African observations, Wright removes himself from his boyhood Mississippi experiences. As I noted previously, Wright was raised poor in a racially hostile environment. *Black Boy* and *American Hunger* tell of his bouts with hunger and deprivation. His comments about the choices that Africans make in order to survive in the colonized country show both his position as an established writer and as a man unwilling to confront how closely conditions in the United States as he knew them parallel those endured by Ghanaians. His reluctance emerges strongly when he observes scantily clad men bringing goods from ships docked off the coast. The men are treated as machinery and receive very little pay for their work. Wright concludes that he would never do that kind of work. This is an astounding declaration from a man who describes the jobs that he took as a desperate child, including one where he received a vicious dog bite, and as an adult during the Great Depression, when pay was meager. What wouldn't a person do to eat and to care for his family? Wright seems inconsistent in his judgment of a people whose choices are not much different from the ones he had to make until he became a successful writer.

In his desire to determine his relationship with Africa, he struggles with his lack of understanding about the people. Wright remains unsatisfied with his communications with Nkrumah. Despite his awareness that the prime minister is in the middle of making a historical political change in Africa, Wright is baffled by what he perceives as his acts of aloofness. Wright seems unwilling to believe that he, himself, is a foreigner and that his status as a writer would, in any country, make a person under international observation wary. This may be why the prime minister does not give Wright notes from his speech or why he does not allow Wright's speech to be given to a reporter—whom Wright does not know—for publication. As a result of this and other conversations he has with African people who appear guarded, Wright dismisses the meaning of his foreign presence by assigning a generalized label: "I found the African an oblique, a hard-to-know man who seemed to take a kind of childish pride in trying to create a state of bewilderment in the presence of strangers" (*BP,* 94). It was their fault, and not any other reason, why he was a "bewildered stranger."

At times, his status as a stranger becomes synonymous with loss. Dr. J. B. Danquah responds to Wright's request to learn more about why he is with the opposition by telling Wright, "Stay longer and you'll feel your race" and that "the knowledge of your race" will come back (*BP,* 241). He does not always know how to respond. Danquah's response is one of many that make Wright feel alienated from the people of the Gold Coast. The question becomes whether he is separated from the country as a result of his national origin or as a result of the life he has lived as a Westerner? Danquah suggests that it is more the former; with more time in Africa, a black American can reconnect with his past.

On several occasions, Wright identifies himself as a descendant of Africa in an effort to resist the label of stranger. At times he perceives himself as an accepted part of the nation. A significant example is when he is asked by a chief to pour a libation. Wright learns how to greet the man in recognition of his status as "father of the people" (*BP,* 273). According to Wright, the chief accepts him, declaring, "You are African" and by extension gives him permission to pour a libation. Wright does not deny this given distinction once offered and follows the chief's instructions to say what's in "your heart" (*BP,* 273). As Wright pours the beer he says that he calls upon "our common ancestors to witness that [he] had come from America," and further, that he "was a stranger who bore no ill-will toward anyone." Wright reiterates the doubleness of the African American experience in the presence of an African ancestral figure. He goes on to engage in the ceremony by asking for blessings of the fields, the women, and the children. After he is done, accordingly, he is given the blessing of his father who tells him that "he did fine" (*BP,* 275). His experience is not only cultural but spiritual, for Wright makes a deliberate connection with the people of the West African nation. This is a rare occasion when he looks beyond himself and expresses hope for the group. Since Wright offers no commentary on his words or those of the chief, we can only assume that this portion of his "record in a land of pathos" was an experience that may have given him an answer to the question about his relationship to Africa. More important, his engagement through a cultural ceremony is distinctly personal. Given the fact that he was abandoned by his father and he has already declared himself a "son of Africa" who has returned, Wright experiences a moment of acceptance that he expresses desire for from his father in *Black Boy, The Outsider,* and other works with and without a father's presence.

Wright ultimately concludes that a return to Africa does not culminate with placement in a home. His insistence that he is Western is honest and realistic. In his problematic interpretations of his observations, which in themselves prove that he has on some level accepted his Western identity, he rejects any romanticizing of Africa. It would seem, then, that his interest in understanding the people and cultures of Ghana as well as his disappointment about his experiences there are similar to his views of his father and the black southern communities of his youth. He won't deny that he is connected to Africa and the black South, but how he feels about that connection is hauntingly complex.

Unlike Richard Wright, Malcolm X is much more optimistic about Africa, declaring political and religious ties with the continent through Islam and the Organization of Afro-American Unity. Of course, it must be noted that the two men emerged from significantly different backgrounds. Malcolm X was raised in a home with parents who kept abreast of African world affairs. As members of the UNIA, they participated in a movement that was based on reuniting with other blacks in Africa and making the continent into a unified nation. Though he speaks more about his father's role as president of the local branch of the UNIA, his brother Wilbert recalls that his Grenadian mother had a major role in exposing them to international affairs by reading from newspapers written by Caribbean activists. He notes, "By reading Garvey's paper and Marryshow's paper, we got an education in international affairs and learned what Black people were doing for their own betterment all over the world."[25] Her presence in the home invited a worldview that inspired her children well into adulthood. Malcolm X's speeches reveal his transformation from a leader in the NOI to a global leader with interests in Africa. In the last year of his life, Malcolm X affirmed an identity as an American who had roots in Africa. He began to engage in conversations with African leaders and to establish a world African movement of blacks under the Organization of Afro-American Unity.

Once Malcolm breaks from the NOI and goes on the Hajj, he is able to construct a global philosophy that is radically different from that of his estranged father figure, Elijah Muhammad. Minister Malcolm tells his followers that Muhammad's interests shifted after his 1960 visit to the East; before then Muhammad was focused on "unity, militancy, and a tendency to be uncompromising."[26] After the visit, he became "more mercenary. More interested in money. More interested in wealth [. . .] more interested in girls."[27] Malcolm goes on to establish himself as one totally dedicated to black folks and the empowerment of black communities by telling the audience that he witnessed Muhammad's dealings with the Ku Klux Klan, which benefited Muhammad and the NOI. Later in the same speech—delivered days after his house was bombed, he believed on orders from Muhammad—he declares that Muhammad "was in the position to unite us with Africa" but did not, telling his audience, "I defy you to find one word in his direct writings that's pro-African."[28] With this speech, he hopes to appeal to the black masses—in Harlem, across the country, and globally—that he has been attempting to unite since his break with Muhammad.

Malcolm is poised to take on the task of uniting black Americans with global black communities after his transition to orthodox Islam. To be sure, his transition from the practices instituted by the NOI is understood. In 1965, Malcolm states that he went to Mecca to make himself "an authentic Muslim" and to educate the Muslims there about the status of "our people who are Muslims."[29] In a speech delivered about two

25. Jan Carew, *Ghosts in Our Blood: With Malcolm X in Africa, England, and the Caribbean,* 116.
26. Bruce Perry, ed., *Malcolm X: The Last Speeches,* 124.
27. Ibid., 125.
28. Ibid., 139.
29. Ibid., 130.

years earlier, on January 23, 1963, he had clarified two points that he seemed to revise by 1965. Speaking on behalf of the Honorable Elijah Muhammad, he made the point that the NOI was not a political organization: "We're not politically inclined or motivated."[30] His other point was that there is no such thing as a liberal white who wants integration; therefore, an integrationist agenda is limiting. He goes on to speak for separation or Black Nationalism where the economy, politics, and society are controlled by blacks. By 1965, his view of these matters has altered, and he publicizes his relationship with civil rights leaders. Notably, one of them is James Farmer, whom he had identified in the January 1963 speech as a "House Negro," making note of his marriage to a white woman. Minister Malcolm also makes clear in this 1965 interview that he is a political leader. His previous statements he attributes to his former mentor: "Notice all of my former statements were prefaced by 'the Honorable Elijah Muhammad teaches thus and so.' They weren't my statements, they were his statements, and I was repeating them."[31] At this point he says that Muhammad has embraced an immoral, corrupt lifestyle and in separating from him, he hopes that broadening his point of view also means that he has elevated himself to a new level of spirituality and global understanding that Muhammad has not reached. Further, bonding with people irrespective of race reflects his move toward spirituality and separation from ideas of racial supremacy.

Once he feels that his religious authenticity has been established, he sets up the Organization of Afro-American Unity in 1964 intent on establishing and maintaining contact with the people of Africa. His travels to the Middle East and to Africa allow him to expand his point of view, which initially perceived all whites as the enemy. He maintains in an interview that "travel does broaden one's soul."[32] Malcolm X makes two extended trips to Africa and the Middle East after his break from the NOI. The first occurs when he travels to Mecca. From there he visits other counties, including Nigeria, Ghana, Liberia, Senegal, Morocco, and Algeria from the end of April to May 21, 1964.[33] While in Africa, he is inspired by the Organization of African Unity (OAU). Founded in

30. Breitman, *By Any Means*, 47.
31. Ibid., 104.
32. Perry, *Speeches*, 91.
33. Malcolm X, *Autobiography*, 377.

1963, the OAU followed a Pan-African philosophy and therefore was in-clusive of all African movements.[34] His later trip occurs between July and November 1964. By then, Malcolm's trajectory in life had led him to the point where he would seek, find, and establish an organization steeped in a Pan-African ideology. He makes the connection between his childhood and adult decisions in *The Autobiography* by linking his early ex-posure to Black Nationalist ideology through his father's participation in Garvey's UNIA. He goes on to note that his involvement with the NOI advanced his childhood observations: "I had been strongly aware of how the Black Nationalist political, economic, and social philosophies had the ability to instill within black men the racial dignity, the incentive, and the confidence that the black race needs today to get off its knees" (*TAMX*, 382). Notably, he gives credit to three men—absent here is his mother and her cultural background as well as her involvement with the UNIA—for leading him to embracing a Pan-African agenda that he hopes will make him a viable international leader. Malcolm X's lack of reference to his mother suggests his insistence that his role as a black leader also affirms his masculine identity as well.

The minister has been criticized for not articulating a clear agenda regarding what process the organization would take to achieve the aim of serving and uniting black communities. Though he has expressed his opposition of Muhammad and many of his teachings, he remains loyal to the idea of black community. In his 1965 speech, his plan of action re-mains vague, but he declares dedication "not for just one religious seg-regation of the community, but for the entire Black community."[35] He goes on to offer Harlem as an example and states that it is up to mem-bers of the community to clean it up and control it. These ideas are not dissimilar from the Black Nationalist ideas that he professed under the leadership of Muhammad. It should be noted here that his break from NOI and more important, his trip to Mecca, mark the first times in his life in which he could command a definition of himself as an influential leader. He believed he could not simply insert himself into the discourse and expect results, he had to move strategically as he was hindered by his former dealings as a Black Muslim. He says, "I had to gradually reshape that image." He notes further, "I was trying to turn a corner," and he had

34. DeCaro, *On the Side*, 226.
35. Perry, *Speeches*, 133.

to keep his anger contained, though he was still as angry as he had been (*TAMX*, 382). The agenda, then, had to be carefully structured according to the needs of the people. That agenda began to grow.

In July 1964 he attends the OAU's conference in Cairo. When he arrives, he publicizes his idea to go to the United Nations to charge the United States with violation of human rights.[36] By 1964, independence movements had begun to change Africa. Ghana received independence in 1957; Nigeria, Niger, Togo, and Senegal gained independence in 1960. The movements that led to these countries achieving independence obviously corresponded with the Civil Rights movement of the United States. Black people in Africa and in the United States felt empowered as evidenced by the progressive historic changes that the world was witnessing. What could happen, then, if they worked together? Malcolm X had come from a family that believed in the power of unified blacks, and he was finally witnessing black people working together. Under the NOI, he had been limited in his activism since the organization was opposed to engaging in politics, meaning that the Civil Rights movement—whether members agreed with the nonviolent tactics or not—was engaging black folks while the Black Muslim movement seemed unwilling to effect change in the black community. Its focus was only on those who joined the organization, while the Civil Rights movement was intent on helping all blacks. This was a point of frustration to Malcolm X and many NOI followers. Small wonder that when he returns to the U.S. and gives his "Declaration of Independence" he willingly extends himself to the Civil Rights movement leaders.

Since blacks are engaged in movements that are positioning them as leaders, Malcolm X, himself a leader, asserts his empowerment as founder of his own movement. When he visits Nigeria in 1964, he says that he sees himself as an Afro-American who is fighting for Constitutional rights in America, but that Afro-Americans should philosophically and culturally "return" to Africa and "develop a working unity in the framework of Pan-Africanism" (*TAMX*, 357). Minister Malcolm defines himself as an American entitled to the rights and privileges of citizenship, in contrast to his statements under NOI when he publicly criticized those who fought for citizenship rights. At this point, he is intent on building the black com-

36. Rodnell Collins, *Seventh Child*, 172.

munity in America. His visit to Africa allows him to see the possibilities of black people working together to achieve a common goal.

Malcolm X is not critical of Africa, likely because he feels embraced by its people. While in Nigeria he says that he is given the name Omowale, meaning "the son has come home," by a Nigerian student organization (*TAMX*, 357). Naming has marked significant identity changes in his life. He exchanged his birth name of Little for X when he accepted NOI. When he converted to orthodox Islam by completing the Hajj he became El Hajj Malik El-Shabazz. This additional name signifies his acceptance by Africans of Nigeria as belonging to them. Notably, here, he has lived the dream of his father who as a member of the UNIA and supported the idea of returning to Africa. Before leaving Nigeria, Malcolm X is asked to join the movement for global empowerment for black people. According to him, a high official tells him that the world will change "the day that African-heritage peoples come together as brothers" (*TAMX*, 358). The minister comments to Haley, "I never had heard that kind of global black thinking from any black man in America" (*TAMX*, 358). He, then, becomes that black man. The official's optimistic declaration undoubtedly serves to inspire his plans for the Organization of Afro-American Unity in the United States.

As Wright had done seven years earlier, Malcolm X visits Ghana, but his observations are significantly different from Wright's. Malcolm was invited to Ghana by African American expatriates, "in collaboration with their allies of the left wing of [Nkrumah's] the Convention People's Party" to "reaffirm their loyalty" to the country's president as to remove the stigma of marginalization.[37] Based on the political situation that also involves Nkrumah dealing with internal divisions, the president does not formally endorse Malcolm X's visit. This may also account for Malcolm's brief reference in *The Autobiography* to having met the president. He provides no details of their conversation. What he seems most impressed by is the feeling of acceptance by these expatriates, a black American community abroad, particularly when he is not sure of his relationship with African Americans. He believes that their welcoming him has to do with his image as a militant black American. Finally, he concludes that he wishes that he could have shared that experience with all black Americans.

37. Gaines, *Americans in Ghana*, 181.

The complex connection that black men feel with Africa, which taxes dual national and cultural identities, as Wright and Hughes show, is one that should not be ignored. But Malcolm X's reaction is significantly different from theirs.

Clearly, he is unable to share his emotions, but telling his story to Haley allows him to give voice to his experience. His is not only the sentiment of having gone to Africa, being given an African name, and having the opportunity to meet with and speak with people who seem to value his experiences; we must also consider the context of this visit. This was not his first visit to Africa. For reasons that are not clear, in *The Autobiography* there is a mere reference to an earlier trip to Africa that he made with Elijah Muhammad. It would seem that that visit would have received quite a bit of attention from a man whose love of black people would have been furthered by his first trip to the continent. We can surmise that the lack of a description allows him to "legitimately" criticize Muhammad later for not establishing a relationship with Africa. However, the second trip occurs when he is trying to firm up an identity that is uniquely his and separate from those of other African American leaders, and it occurs when he has left the United States in the midst of his public break from Muhammad. It stands to reason then that he chooses not to criticize Muhammad for a number of reasons, one being his desire not to shift the focus away from his visit and on to his relationship with a man who has a more established following.

Malcolm X's trip to Ghana also gives him an opportunity to look at the presence of women in society. While in Ghana, he meets the widow of Du Bois, Shirley, then the director of Ghanian television. In a 1965 interview he gives in America, he honors her position by offering her status in Ghana as an example to African American women, stating that they should be "mighty proud."[38] He goes on to deem her as one of the "most intelligent women [he'd] ever met."[39] His observations of her allow him to see and comment upon the impressive technology she uses. He concludes that the technology, in her hands, is only one aspect of Ghana that he found impressive. This revelation is given in response to his impressions of Ghana in general and not in response to a question about the status of women in Africa. Ghana, he believes, is "progres-

38. Perry, *Speeches*, 96.
39. Ibid.

sive."[40] Malcolm X proves again his ability to transform. Unlike in *The Autobiography*, in this interview he proves his ability to regard women as intelligent beings, capable of contributing to the progress of a developing country. If African American women are to see Mrs. Du Bois as a model, then they too can engage in such work if the opportunity arises in the United States.

The Autobiography of Malcolm X allows Malcolm X to reveal layers of himself. When Haley approaches him and Malcolm agrees to tell his story, his intent to expose others to the teaching of Elijah Muhammad is no secret. Once Muhammad and Malcolm X become estranged, Malcolm alludes to his desire to shed his old image and to produce a new one. His final transition to orthodox Islam and his ascent to international leader both result from a lifetime of engagements with black communities and organizations in the United States. It would seem that his trip to Mecca and his trip to Africa allow him to make peace with himself as a black man in the United States. He reaches a spiritual point of satisfaction and complements his spiritual status with a cultural identity. Ultimately, Malcolm's "return" to the "fatherland" allows him to reclaim the legacy of the identity that his father wanted him to have. Thus, he successfully engages the process of healing the loss of his father—a loss that has led this son of activists on a circular journey to become an internationally recognized activist in his own right.

Barack Obama's relationship to Africa differs significantly from that of the other three black men. Obama goes to Kenya intent on learning more about his father and his father's culture, and as a result, he hopes to heal the scars left by his father's abandonment of him. He admits that he feels his sense of emptiness can be alleviated by visiting Africa.[41] As a consequence of feeling rejected by his father, he is apprehensive about going to Kenya, even though he has an established relationship with his half-sister, Auma, and has met his half-brother, Roy. Nevertheless, he poses questions about his acceptability, one of the more significant being: "What if, . . . his leaving me behind meant nothing, and the only tie that bound me to him, or to Africa, was a name, a blood type, or white people's scorn?" (*DFMF,* 302). This is a loaded question. His is a desire to feel acceptance or a connection to Africa by way of Kenya as part of the

40. Ibid.
41. Obama, *Dreams from My Father,* 302.

community Luo. Obama has a direct association with Africa unlike the majority of American-born people of African descent whose relationship to Africa involves a broader identification with West Africa that does not include the details of ancestral relationships. Despite this, he still fears the possibility of experiencing typically impersonalized African American identification with Africa.

His visit to Kenya allows him to meet many relatives from several generations. Readers accustomed to "traditional Western" families, where the children are raised by their biological parents, may have trouble following the relations of the Obama family. A close reading reveals that Obama's father and his sister, Sara, were raised by Grannie, the second wife of Obama's grandfather, Onyango. Kezia is Obama Sr.'s first wife by traditional ceremony, and she, Auma, and Roy were left behind when Obama Sr. went to the United States to pursue his education. Besides meeting all of them, Obama also meets his biological grandmother, Akuma, who reportedly abandoned her son, Obama Sr., and her daughter, Sara, when they were small children.

It is from Grannie and other relatives that he learns about his paternal history. Obama reveals a great deal about his grandfather, Onyango, who, Barack's mother has always told him, did not want Obama Sr. to marry the white American woman. Barack learns what he can only learn by "returning" to home square—that his grandfather spent time learning the ways of the colonial system and brought many of those ways into his home with the expectation that his wives would follow his instructions. When they, especially Akuma, were not successful, he punished them. His training derived from his experience as a cook to a British captain. According to Grannie through the translation of Auma and through Obama's (re)storytelling, Onyango was a man who sought Europeans as models because he had come to believe that they were "always improving themselves" and that Africans would never accomplish anything unless they were beaten (*DFMF,* 406).

Prior to hearing his grandmother talk about his grandfather, he had conjured an image of him based on the scanty information he received from his mother and her family. He reveals that he had surmised that his grandfather was "a cruel man," but "an independent man, a man of his people, opposed to white rule" (*DFMF,* 406). He realizes that he cobbled together this image based only on the facts that his grandfather opposed his son's marriage to Barack's mother because of her race and that he is Muslim, which Barack linked with the Nation of Islam. Grannie's stories cause him to think of his grandfather negatively as an "Uncle Tom. Collaborator. House Nigger" (*DFMF,* 406).

He answers his insecurities about his grandfather when he proceeds with his grandmother's "story" (note here her story is retold by him). She reveals that he was influenced by European ways but remained loyal to Luo traditions such as "respect for elders, respect for authority, and order and custom in all his affairs" (*DFMF,* 407). Though he converted to Christianity for a while and changed his last name, he returned to his Islamic beliefs. The intimidating man for whom Barack is searching emerges later in the story when she characterizes him as a fearless man who took on disrespectful neighbors and a threatening shaman.

His grandmother gives him information about the relationship between his father and his grandfather that may help him to understand his father's paternal weaknesses. It is possible that Obama Sr. had harsh feelings against his mother for abandoning him and accepted Grannie as his mother, though his sister rejected Grannie as her mother. His relationship with his father was continuous. She reports, "Although he did not show it, your grandfather was also very fond of Barack, because the boy was so clever" (*DFMF,* 414). This is the introduction of a pattern of Obama Sr.'s conflicts with his father. In fact, Onyango eventually tells Obama Sr. that he will not amount to anything because of his mischievous behavior in defiance of his father's authority and the authority of others. At one point, he is expelled from school, beaten bloody by Onyango, and sent to take a job. Obama Sr. loses the job and is met with more of his father's scorn. When he is arrested for attending political meetings about independence, his father does not bail him out of jail. Eventually he marries, impresses two American teachers, and is admitted to the University of Hawaii.

Perhaps more important, Obama learns what may be the truth about his family's reaction to learning of his father's decision to marry a white American woman. His grandfather, who may also have been married to a European woman during his travels with the British, was opposed to his father not "behaving responsibly" (*DFMF,* 422). He questioned how Obama Sr. would continue to meet his responsibilities to his family in Kenya. Further, he asked if his white American wife would return to Africa and live as a Luo wife, which would mean accepting his previous wife and children. Though his father did marry his mother against their wishes, Barack discovers that his family was happy that Barack Jr. was born. What he probably most cherishes is that acceptance as an Obama came with his birth. Based on his father's return without his American wife, Onyango's concerns proved legitimate. Obama relays this family history by detaching himself from it and reporting it without overt interpretation or comment. He does not reveal his feelings about the details, in contrast to his usual openness regarding his interpretations of his own behavior and that of his maternal family members.

His tone remains detached as he (re)tells what he learns about relationships between Luo men and women from his grandmother. Clearly, Obama Sr. learned a great deal about women from his father. His sister is not allowed to advance in education since she is expected to marry a man who will take care of her. When he and his sister are still young, Obama Sr. leaves a school, citing his teacher's gender as the reason. He has already been taught that women are second to men and even to boys. In his adult life he moves from one wife to another, marrying at least three times. Kezia, his first wife, is the only one who remains a constant presence in his life, but as Barack surmises, his mother remains in love with his father until his death. His last wife is bitter and discourages her son from having a relationship with any of the rest of her ex-husband's children.

Obama Sr.'s relationships with his wives and his estranged children have a profound effect on all of his children. Despite Onyango's relationship with his son and his strict ways, he did not abandon his children. In fact, Obama Sr. and Sara were found dirty and starving while on their way to find the mother who had abandoned them. Their father took them back and ensured that they were cared for. Obama Sr. seems unable to form meaningful relationships that will result in well-cared-for families. It also seems as though every phase of his life is marked by a new marriage, and the most successful phases are marked by his marriages to white women. While in the midst of disappointing his father in Kenya, he marries Kezia. When he begins his education in America, he marries Obama's mother. His return to Africa to begin a new job in government is followed by his marriage to another white American woman. During his fall from his position, he returns to Kezia. Finally, when he is back in government again, he has another relationship that results in a new child.

Though Barack's father leaves a lot to be desired as a father, Obama Sr. is admired for his generosity and known for giving money to relatives. Barack is told one story of his father giving people who were waiting for public transportation a free ride in his car. At other times he was known to buy drinks for men who frequented the same bar as he. Auma notes that he tried desperately to hold onto the idea that his name meant so much to people that even when he did not have the money to buy items, they would give them to him anyway. To allow him his dignity, she did not confront him on this matter and instead helped him to maintain the belief. His father was abandoned by the people to whom he had been generous after he lost his job for criticizing the Kenya government, but when his father was reinstated, he once again was generous to those who had not been to him. Barack is able to understand his father's complexity. In these stories he appears to be a man who loved good times, enjoyed helping people, and was loyal to family, friends, and those in need. Obama does not offer commentary. Instead he lets the oral tradition of storytelling prevail. The integration of storytelling does not just allow him to mask his feelings about the story itself; it also lets him engage in this tradition by keeping the words as "hers" even though he is actually (re)telling the story.

Barack may learn more about his father and grandfather, but he also learns more about what it means to belong to an African family. He remarks on how he is constantly surrounded by relatives who feel it rude to leave him alone when Auma is away at work. He is constantly bombarded by requests for money and gifts from America. He observes the conditions in which his aunt lives as she cares for the less-fortunate members of their extended family. More notably, he finds himself being asked to take a side regarding the inheritance of his father's children and other dependents. In particular, his biological grandmother denies the paternity of one of the sons his father claims by Kezia, and she feels more entitled to the inheritance than Grannie.

Belonging to the Obama family has many implications. Before he leaves Kenya he is identified as a Luo and as an Obama. When he arrives at the airport, he is identified by a woman who knows his name and knew his father. Her recognition makes him feel immediately accepted into the community, as his name has a meaning in Kenya, whereas in America he finds himself having to account for his name, its meaning, and his history. As he shops in the market, he tells a woman that he is Luo. Further, in order to get back his lost luggage, his sister identifies an "uncle" who had a relationship with their father. The "uncle" uses his influence to make a call, and Obama is able to retrieve his luggage.

Ultimately, Barack's trip to Africa helps him to achieve his aim. He leaves having answered the questions about his identity raised by his father's absence from his life. He learns that he is a welcomed part of his father's family and that they see him as having been away from home. His return to them allows him to claim an identity that gives him a cultural connection to the Luo traditions. Most of all, he is able to connect with his father through the stories of his Grannie, a Luo elder. It is clear that the autobiographical Obama "I" is searching for a home, a place where he is accepted as part of the community without having to reason why he should be part of the community. His home/community is also a healing place. The autobiography ends with his locating himself at his father's grave to grieve his father's death and his loss, feelings he was not able to access upon hearing of his father's death. Thus, the grave represents a healing ground for him. Obama has established a place of belonging in his father's land.

Africa has different meanings to African Americans. To some it is a land of their cultural and perhaps racial origins; to others it may be just another place where people of no particular significance reside. The varying perceptions of Africa among the African American men I have discussed—Langston Hughes, Richard Wright, Malcolm X, and Barack Obama—prove that experiences may be shared, but they are not completely imitated. What they certainly do make clear as a result of their personal journeys and written reactions is that they all went in search of a deeper understanding of themselves as men of African descent. For each man to be descended from those who were removed from the continent by whatever means and to have returned as a "son," in the words of Wright, is an expression of the self that longs to know where that self belongs. The journey, then, is a return to the double-conscious self that exists in a state of striving. Hughes sees himself and those Africans fighting for justice as united by a common political experience in the twentieth century, if not at least connected by a racial bond. Wright concludes that he is too Western to identify as he may wish with Africa. Malcolm X feels an acceptance based on a kinship and on his political beliefs. Obama literally finds his father's home and calls it his own. The return is met with a challenge that American history distorts, but the return is never an ending. It is a beginning that marks continuous growth, understanding, and healing.

Conclusion

Contemporary African American Fathers and Communities

Similar to twentieth-century black male autobiographers I've discussed, twenty-first century black male autobiographers have faced fatherlessness in black communities. One example is Michael Datcher's *Raising Fences: A Black Man's Love Story* (2001). The autobiography begins with the black male subject wondering about the identity of an absent father even though he has a loving mother and siblings. Datcher focuses on his experiences in the black communities in Los Angeles. Another compelling work is *The Pact* (2002), written by Sampson Davis, George Jenkins, and Rameck Hunt, with Lisa Frazier. The "autobiography" combines the stories of three young men from working-class neighborhoods who decide together that they will attend, and graduate from, medical school. Readers learn about the absence of fathers, the presence of the community, and the men's move from uncertain futures to successful careers as medical doctors.

Beyond the autobiographical texts, the media has provided portraits of fathers in the home. One of the most recent and well-known black father-and-son relationships is that of Theo and Heathcliff in the popular *Cosby Show*. The first episode features Cliff talking with his son about his less-than-acceptable grades. After Theo renders a heartfelt monologue to his father about the importance of his accepting his son with all of his flaws, Cliff tells him that he brought him into the world and he will take him out. One of the more memorable episodes of the show may be one in which Theo's parents discover that their son has come into possession of a joint. When confronted, he tells them that it is not his, and they tell him that they believe him. Theo, wanting to make sure they believe him, tracks down the owner of the drug and talks him into confessing his culpability to Claire and Cliff. The show ends with their reminding him of how much they trust him.

The Cosby Show was criticized as inauthentic in its portrayal of a black family. Was it because there were a father and a mother in a home, and they managed to raise children who seemed to escape societal pressures and racialized confrontations? Criticism of the lack of race portrayal by these black actors also suggests that there is a lack of authenticity in the depiction of a black professional man who loves his son, his wife, and his family. Ultimately, as entertaining as the show was, black male autobiographers from Olaudah Equiano to Michael Datcher challenge these wishful notions that black children can mature without feeling the challenges of racial prejudices.

What was most certainly lacking in *The Cosby Show* was the presence of a black community. Bill Cosby, over a decade removed from his role of Heathcliff Huxtable, spoke at an event commemorating the fiftieth anniversary of *Brown vs. the Topeka Board of Education* about the problems of black communities. His comments became controversial, partly because they were regarded as insulting to African Americans and partly because he chose to make them at a public event. However, many applauded Cosby's point. He reiterated his message, which concerned fathering, at subsequent events: "I want you to go back to parenting. You young men, when you get married and you have children, you've got to parent. You've got to be parents."[1] To give credence to his call to black parents, he joined with Alvin Poussaint to expose problems and offer solutions.

Before the publication of Cosby and Poussaint's book, *Come on, People*, and shortly after the infamous speech made at the NAACP commemoration, Michael Eric Dyson issued a response. Dyson argues that Bill Cosby had actually perpetuated stereotypes about poor black folks. I mention the Cosby-Dyson "debate" to illuminate the significance of dissent between two black fathers of sons, both of whom have doctoral degrees and both of whom come from humble beginnings. Emerging from the two men are varying degrees of how to solve the problems that exist

---

1. Bill Cosby and Alvin Poussaint, interview by Tim Russert, Oct. 14, 2007, *Meet the Press*, http://www.msnbac.msn.com/id/21293963/.

among black families. Cosby argues that African Americans must take more responsibility for uplifting themselves, and if they do not, they should not be surprised when life does not bear pleasant fruit. Dyson, on the other hand, argues that not all African Americans are doomed and that America is not in the best shape. This debate raises questions posed by E. Franklin Frazier in the early twentieth century: Who's to blame for the weaknesses of black families: whites, blacks, or both?

Regardless of what we believe the answer to be, both Dyson and Cosby inspire us to look honestly at the present state of black communities. There are currently national initiatives that encourage fathers to have relationships with their children. The National Father Initiative reported in 2002 that "thirty-four percent of children live in homes without their biological father—including 66 percent of black children, 35 percent of Hispanic children and 27 percent of white children." Those statistics are bleak, but they pose yet another question—whether the children in these homes have relationships with their fathers. Our autobiographers have proven that having that relationship and feeling accepted as the son of the father is of the utmost importance.

If we look beyond mere statistics and listen to the voices, black men's autobiographies certainly speak to the struggles that may occur when any boy, regardless of race, does not have a strong relationship with his father. More important, however, they also prove that not having a relationship with one's father is not a formula for certain doom. Hughes and Wright became, and remain today, internationally known writers. Though largely misunderstood, Malcolm X's accomplishments and potential as an international leader are still recognized today.

And, as this book goes to press, Obama is president-elect of the United States of America—a historic feat for an African American. In *Dreams,* Obama refers to older African Americans who express their concern for his decision to become a community activist rather than a corporate employee. His choice to pursue the former set him on the path that would take him to the White House. His achievement is remarkable not only because he identifies as an African American, making this a momentous event for all Americans, but also because he was reared in the United States without a father. Obama's victory emerges as an answer to many of the questions posed in his autobiography. One of the most significant asks, What is the role of an African American male in post–Civil Rights America? Obama's answer: The African American male can define that on his own terms. Their success does not mean that fatherlessness does not have an impact on self-perception. It does mean that the love of families and the support of communities can contribute to the healthy growth of fatherless children. Indeed, American communities can produce socially productive black men. It is never too late to begin the process of healing.

Works Cited

Ako, Edward. "Langston Hughes and the Négritude Movement: A Study in Literary Influences." *College Language Association Journal* 28 (1984): 46–56.

Amos, John. "Black Like Obama: What the Junior Illinois Senator's Appearance on the National Scene Reveals about Race in America, and Where We Should Go from Here." *Thurgood Marshall Law Review* 31.1 (Fall 2005): 79–100. *General OneFile.* Gale. Northern Arizona University–AULC. Sept. 30, 2007.

Barrett, Lindon. "The Gaze of Langston Hughes: Subjectivity, Homoeroticism, and the Feminine in *The Big Sea.*" *Yale Journal of Criticism: Interpretation in the Humanities* 12:2 (1999 Fall): 383–97.

Bassoff, Evelyn. *Between Mothers and Sons: The Making of Vital and Loving Men.* New York: Penguin Books, 1994.

Blassingame, John. *Slave Community: Plantation Life in the Antebellum South.* Rev. ed. New York: Oxford University Press, 1979.

Blassingame, John, and Mary Frances Berry. *Long Memory: The Black Experience in America.* New York: Oxford University Press, 1982.

Booker, Christopher B. *"I Will Wear No Chain!" A Social History of African American Males.* Westport, CT: Praeger, 2000.

Borden, Anne. "Heroic 'Hussies' and 'Brilliant Queers': Genderracial Resistance in the Works of Langston Hughes." *African American Review* 28:3 (1994 Fall): 333–45.

Boyd, Herb, and Robert L. Allen. *Brotherman: The Odyssey of Black Men in America.* New York: Ballantine Books, 1995.

Breitman, George, ed. *By Any Means Necessary: Speeches, Interviews, and Letters by Malcolm X.* New York: Pathfinder, 1970.

Brown, Stephanie, and Keith Clark. "Melodramas of Beset Black Manhood? Meditations on African American Masculinity as Scholarly Topos and Social Menace: An Introduction." *Callaloo* 26.3 (2003): 732–37.

Butterfield, Stephen. *Black Autobiography in America.* Amherst: University of Massachusetts Press, 1974.

Carby, Hazel V. *Race Men.* Cambridge: Harvard University Press, 1998.

Carew, Jan. *Ghosts in Our Blood: With Malcolm X in Africa, England, and the Caribbean.* New York: Lawrence Hill Books, 1994.

Chiwengo, Ngwarsungu. "Richard Wright's Africa." In *Richard Wright's Travel Writings: New Reflections,* edited by Virginia Whatley Smith. Jackson: University Press of Mississippi, 2001.

Clark, Keith. *Black Manhood in James Baldwin, Ernest J. Gaines, and August Wilson.* Urbana: University of Illinois Press, 2002.

Clegg, Claude. *An Original Man: The Life and Times of Elijah Muhammad.* New York: St. Martin's Press, 1997.

Collins, Patricia Hill. *Black Feminist Thought.* Routledge: Routledge, Chapman and Hall, 1991.

Collins, Rodnell, and A. Peter Bailey. *Seventh Child: A Family Memoir of Malcolm X.* Secaucus, NJ: Carol Publishing Group, 1998.

Conner, Michael E., and Joseph L. White, eds. *Black Fathers: An Invisible Presence in America.* Manwah, NJ: Lawrence Erlbaum, 2006.

Cosby, Bill, and Alvin F. Poussaint. *Come on, People: On the Path from Victims to Victors.* Nashville: Thomas Nelson, 2007.

DeCaro, Louis A., Jr. *On the Side of My People: A Religious Life of Malcolm X.* New York: New York University Press, 1996.

Dixon, Melvin. *Ride Out the Wilderness: Geography and Identity in Afro-American Literature.* Urbana: University of Illinois Press, 1987.

Du Bois, W. E. B. "Of Our Spiritual Strivings." *The Souls of Black Folk.* New York: Penguin Books, 1989.

Dudley, David L. *My Father's Shadow: Intergenerational Conflict in African American Men's Autobiography.* Philadelphia: University of Pennsylvania Press, 1991.

Dyson, Michael Eric. *Making Malcolm: The Myth and Meaning of Malcolm X.* New York: Oxford University Press, 1995.

———. *Is Bill Cosby Right? Or Has the Black Middle Class Lost Its Mind?* New York: Basic Civitas, 2005.

Emanuel, James A. "The Christ and the Killers." In *Langston Hughes: Critical Perspectives Past and Present*, edited by Henry Louis Gates Jr. and K. A. Appiah. New York: Amistad, 1993.

Equiano, Olaudah. *The Interesting Narrative of Olaudah Equiano, or Gustavas Vassa*, edited by Robert Allison. Boston: Bedford, 1995.

Fabre, Michael. *The Unfinished Quest of Richard Wright*. Translated by Isabel Barzan. New York: William Morrow, 1973.

Felgar, Robert. *Understanding Richard Wright's "Black Boy": A Student Casebook to Issues, Sources, and Historical Documents*. Westport, CT: Greenwood, 1998.

Ferguson, Andrew. "The Literary Obama: From Eloquent Memoir to Democratic Boilerplate." Review of *Dreams from My Father: A Story of Race and Inheritance* by Barack Obama and *The Audacity of Hope: Thoughts on Reclaiming the American Dream* by Barack Obama. *Weekly Standard* 12.21 (Feb. 12, 2007): NA. *General OneFile*. Gale. Northern Arizona University–AULC. Sept. 26, 2007.

Frazier, E. Franklin. *The Negro Family in the United States*. Chicago: University of Chicago Press, 1939.

Gaines, Kevin Kelley. *Americans in Ghana: Black Expatriates and the Civil Rights Movement*. Chapel Hill: University of North Carolina Press, 2006.

Gilroy, Paul. *The Black Atlantic: Modernity and Double Consciousness*. Cambridge: Harvard University Press, 1993.

Griffin, Farah Jasmine. "Ironies of the Saint": Malcolm X, Black Women, and the Price of Protection. In *Sisters in the Struggle*, edited by Bettye Collier-Thomas and V. P. Franklin, New York: New York University Press, 2001.

Harris, Trudier. "Native Sons and Foreign Daughters." In *New Essays on Richard Wright*, edited by Keneth Kinnamon. New York: Cambridge University Press, 1990.

———. *Exorcising Blackness: Historical and Literary Lynching and Burning Rituals*. Bloomington: Indiana University Press, 1984.

Hughes, Langston, *The Big Sea*. New York: Hill and Wang, 1940.

———. *Not without Laughter*. New York: Macmillan, 1969.

———. "Father and Son." *The Ways of White Folks*. New York: Vintage, 1990.

———."Cross." In *The Collected Poems of Langston Hughes*, edited by Arnold Rampersad. New York: Alfred A. Knopf, 1994.

————. Langston Hughes Papers. Yale University Collection of American Literature, Beinecke Rare Book and Manuscript Library.

————."The Twenties: Harlem and Its Negritude." In *The Collected Works of Langston Hughes: Essays on Art, Race, Politics, and World Affairs,* edited by Chris C. De Santis. Columbia: University of Missouri Press, 2002.

Jacobs, Harriet. *Incidents in the Life of a Slave Girl.* In *Norton Anthology of African American Literature,* edited by Henry Louis Gates Jr. and Nellie McKay. New York: Norton, 1997.

JanMohamed, Abdul R. *The Death-Bound-Subject: Richard Wright's Archeology of Death.* Durham: Duke University Press, 2005.

Kestleoot, Lilyan. "Negritude and Its American Sources." In *Black Writers in French: A Literary History of Negritude,* translated by Ellen Conroy Kennedy. Washington, DC: Howard University Press, 1991.

Kinnamon, Keneth, and Michel Fabre, eds. *Conversations with Richard Wright.* Jackson: University of Mississippi Press, 1993.

Loftus, Brian. "In/Verse Autobiography: Sexual (In)Difference and the Textual Backside of Langston Hughes's *The Big Sea." A/B: Auto/Biography Studies* 15:1 (2000): 141–61.

Madhubuti, Haki R. *Tough Notes: A Healing Call for Creating Exceptional Black Men.* Chicago: Third World, 2002.

Marable, Manning. Radio interview. Monday, February 21, 2005. "The Undiscovered Malcolm X: Stunning New Info on the Assassination, His Plans to Unite the Civil Rights and Black Nationalist Movements and the Three 'Missing' Chapters from His Autobiography." http://www.democracynow.org/2005/2/21/ the undiscovered malcolm x stunning new.

Marriot, David. *On Black Men.* New York: Columbia University Press, 2000.

McCall, Dan. *The Example of Richard Wright.* New York: Harcourt, Brace, and World, 1969.

·Miller, R. Baxter. "The Physics of Change in 'Father and Son.'" In *Langston Hughes: The Man, His Art, and His Continuing Influence. Critical Studies in Black Life and Culture,* 29, edited by C. James Trotman. New York: Garland, 1995.

Morrison, Toni. "The Site of Memory." In *Inventing the Truth: The Art and Craft of Memories,* edited by William Zinsser. Boston: Houghton Mifflin, 1987.

Mostern, Kenneth. *Autobiography and Black Identity Politics: Racialization in Twentieth-Century America.* New York: Cambridge University Press, 1999.

Obama, Barack. *Dreams from my Father: A Story of Race and Inheritance.* New York: Three Rivers, 2004.

———. *The Audacity of Hope: Thoughts on Reclaiming the American Dream.* Edinburgh: Canongate, 2007.

Olney, James. *Metaphors of Self: The Meaning of Autobiography.* Princeton: Princeton University Press, 1972.

Olney, James, ed. "Some Versions of Memory/Some Versions of Bios: The Ontology of Autobiography." In *Autobiography: Essays Theoretical and Critical.* Princeton: Princeton University Press, 1980.

Perry, Bruce, ed. *Malcolm X: The Last Speeches.* New York: Pathfinder, 1989.

Raboteau, Albert. *A Fire in the Bones: Reflections on African-American Religious History.* Beacon Press: Boston, 1995.

Rampersad, Arnold. *The Life of Langston Hughes, Volume 1: 1902–1941.* New York: Oxford University Press: 1986.

Rampersad, Arnold, ed. *The Collected Poems of Langston Hughes.* New York: Alfred A. Knopf, 1994.

Rickford, Russell. *Betty Shabazz: A Remarkable Story of Survival and Faith before and after Malcolm X.* Naperville, IL: Sourcebooks, 2003.

Rowley, Hazel. *Richard Wright: The Life and Times.* New York: Henry Holt, 2001.

Sanders, Herman A. *Daddy, We Need You Now! A Primer on African-American Male Socialization.* New York: University Press of America, 1996.

Schultz, Elizabeth. "Natural and Unnatural Circumstances in Langston Hughes' *Not Without Laughter.*" *Callaloo* 25.4 (2002) 1177–87.

Smith, Marcia. "Marcus Garvey: Look for Me in the Whirlwind." Produced and directed by Stanley Nelson. *American Experience.* PBS, 2001.

Tate, Claudia. *Psychoanalysis and Black Novels: Desire and the Protocol of the Race.* New York: Oxford, 1998.

Webb, Constance. *Richard Wright: A Biography.* New York: Putnam, 1968.

Williams, Roland, Jr. *African American Autobiography and the Quest for Freedom.* Westport, CT: Greenwood Press, 2000.

Williams, Sherley Anne. "Papa Dick and Sister-Woman: Reflections on Women in the Fiction of Richard Wright." In *American Novelists*

Revisited: Essays in Feminine Criticism, edited by Fritz Fleischman. Boston: G. K. Hall, 1982.

Wright, Richard. "Fire and Cloud." In *Uncle Tom's Children,* edited by Arnold Rampersad. New York: HarperPerennial, 1993.

———. *The Outsider,* edited by Arnold Rampersad. New York: Harper-Perennial, 1993.

———. Review of *The Big Sea.* In *Langston Hughes: Critical Perspectives Past and Present,* edited by Henry Louis Gates Jr. and K. A. Appiah. New York: Amistad, 1993.

———. *Black Power: A Record of Reactions in a Land of Pathos.* New York: HarperPerennial, 1995.

———. Richard Wright Papers. Yale University Collection of American Literature, Beinecke Rare Book and Manuscript Library.

X, Malcolm. *The Autobiography of Malcolm X,* with the assistance of Alex Haley. New York: Grove, 1965.

X, Malcolm. The Malcolm X Collection: Papers. Manuscripts, Archives, and Rare Books Division. Schomburg Center for Research in Black Culture. New York Public Library. Astor, Lenox and Tilden Foundations.

Yukins, Elizabeth. "The Business of Patriarchy: Black Paternity and Illegitimate Economies in Richard Wright's *The Long Dream.*" *Modern Fiction Studies* 49 (2003): 746–79.

Zeff, Lisa. "Malcolm X: A Search for Identity." *Biography: Men of Distinction.* Executive producer, Lisa Zeff. Produced by ABC News Productions in association with A&E Network, 1999.

Index